Tricia Rhodes's *The Wired Soul* is a beautifully written book for digital immigrants, natives and second-generation net-surfers. She uses the four movements of *Lectio Divina* to invite the reader to unplug, slow down, single-task, and begin to override unhealthy behavioral habits, settling into a leisurely, transformative relationship with God.

**GARY W. MOON**
Executive director of the Martin Institute and Dallas Willard Center, Westmont College; author of *Apprenticeship with Jesus*

Technology is like a present: It can be either a gift or bait. Here is a book mature in wisdom and rich in interactive resources to help us discern what augmentations enhance life and what amputations drain away the blood and reduce the soul to stubs of ones and zeros.

**LEONARD SWEET**
Bestselling author (leonardsweet.com), professor (Drew University, George Fox University, Tabor College), and founder of preachthestory.com

Like so many others, I long for a more contemplative life. I know it's in my best interest. Yet my desire and my experience, born out of my choices, don't often seem to be on the friendliest of terms. Rhodes offers a practical (yes!), fascinating, and insightful set of explanations, encouragement, and tools. This is a *useful* book, very much worth digesting.

**MARK OESTREICHER**
Partner at The Youth Cartel, author of *A Parent's Guide to Understanding Teenage Brains*

*The Wired Soul* helped me identify the ways in which being chronically "connected" interferes with my connection to the One who matters most. Without condemnation, Rhodes's personal observations, appeal to neurological research, and doable spiritual practices challenge and equip readers to reconnect, or connect for the first time, to our Source. Rhodes's prophetic analysis of the modern challenges we all face and her wise life-giving prescription are good gifts to the Church.

**MARGOT STARBUCK**
Author of *Not Who I Imagined*

Human beings are made in the image of a God who is spiritually balanced in a hyper-connected world. With a smartphone in one hand and the findings of cognitive neuroscience in the other, Tricia Rhodes helps the digitally distracted find their spiritual equilibrium again.

**JOHN VAN SLOTEN**
Author of *The Day Metallica Came to Church*

Thank you, Tricia, for lovingly inviting us to take the sugar-filled pacifier called technology out of our mouths before it completely rots our roots and destroys our ability to chew, savor, and swallow what our souls genuinely crave much more than the things that our extremely tech-saturated culture compels us to consume. Your masterful modernization of ancient spiritual practices will undoubtedly transform a digital revolution into a soulful renewal for all of your readers. Thanks for helping us fulfill our joyful destiny of an intimate walk with Jesus.

**STEPHEN MACCHIA**
Founder and president of Leadership Transformations, director of the Pierce Center at Gordon-Conwell Theological Seminary, and author of *Becoming a Healthy Church*

*Mackenzie,*
*Be still and know...*
*In His love,*
*Tricia*

# THE WIRED SOUL

## FINDING SPIRITUAL BALANCE
## IN A HYPERCONNECTED AGE

### TRICIA McCARY RHODES, PhD

A NavPress resource published in alliance
with Tyndale House Publishers, Inc.

# NAVPRESS

NavPress is the publishing ministry of The Navigators, an international Christian organization and leader in personal spiritual development. NavPress is committed to helping people grow spiritually and enjoy lives of meaning and hope through personal and group resources that are biblically rooted, culturally relevant, and highly practical.

**For more information, visit www.NavPress.com.**

*The Wired Soul: Finding Spiritual Balance in a Hyperconnected Age*

Copyright © 2016 by Tricia McCary Rhodes. All rights reserved.

A NavPress resource published in alliance with Tyndale House Publishers, Inc.

*NAVPRESS* and the NAVPRESS logo are registered trademarks of NavPress, The Navigators, Colorado Springs, CO. *TYNDALE* is a registered trademark of Tyndale House Publishers, Inc. Absence of ® in connection with marks of NavPress or other parties does not indicate an absence of registration of those marks.

Published in association with the literary agency of The Steve Laube Agency, LLC.

The Team:
Don Pape, Publisher; David Zimmerman, Acquiring Editor; Jen Phelps, Designer

Unless otherwise indicated, all Scripture quotations are taken from *The Holy Bible*, English Standard Version® (ESV®), copyright © 2001 by Crossway, a publishing ministry of Good News Publishers. Used by permission. All rights reserved.

Scripture quotations marked HCSB are taken from the Holman Christian Standard Bible,® copyright © 1999, 2000, 2002, 2003, 2009 by Holman Bible Publishers. Used by permission. Holman Christian Standard Bible,® Holman CSB,® and HCSB® are federally registered trademarks of Holman Bible Publishers.

Scripture quotations marked MSG are taken from *THE MESSAGE* by Eugene H. Peterson, copyright © 1993, 1994, 1995, 1996, 2000, 2001, 2002. Used by permission of NavPress Publishing Group. All rights reserved.

Scripture quotations marked NASB are taken from the New American Standard Bible,® copyright © 1960, 1962, 1963, 1968, 1971, 1972, 1973, 1975, 1977, 1995 by The Lockman Foundation. Used by permission.

Scripture quotations marked NIV are taken from the Holy Bible, *New International Version,*® NIV.® Copyright © 1973, 1978, 1984, 2011 by Biblica, Inc.® Used by permission. All rights reserved worldwide.

Some of the anecdotal illustrations in this book are true to life and are included with the permission of the persons involved. All other illustrations are composites of real situations, and any resemblance to people living or dead is coincidental.

Library of Congress Cataloging-in-Publication Data

Names: Rhodes, Tricia McCary, author.
Title: The wired soul : finding spiritual balance in a hyperconnected age / Tricia McCary Rhodes, PhD.
Description: Colorado Springs : NavPress, 2016. | Includes bibliographical references.
Identifiers: LCCN 2016015628 (print) | LCCN 2016016497 (ebook) | ISBN 9781631465123 | ISBN 9781631465154 (Apple) | ISBN 9781631465130 (E-Pub) | ISBN 9781631465147 ( Kindle)
Subjects: LCSH: Spiritual life—Christianity.
Classification: LCC BV4501.3 .R463 2016 (print) | LCC BV4501.3 (ebook) | DDC 248—dc23
LC record available at https://lccn.loc.gov/2016015628

Printed in the United States of America

| 22 | 21 | 20 | 19 | 18 | 17 | 16 |
|----|----|----|----|----|----|----|
| 7  | 6  | 5  | 4  | 3  | 2  | 1  |

To my grandsons, Dane and Roman, true digital natives.
You were in the back of my mind with every page I wrote.

# CONTENTS

# CHAPTER 01

# WIRED SOULS
# IN A DIGITAL WORLD

THE MIDDAY SUN cast a golden glow across the meadow where I played with my brothers and sisters, our squeals and laughter peppering the air amidst a chorus of raucous birdsong. It was Saturday afternoon. My father, a nightshift oil refinery worker, had a rare day off, so we'd set out—seven of us packed like sardines into our two-door Ford Coupe—to waste time driving about the countryside. With no destination in mind, no schedule to keep, we just drove right out of our suburban neighborhood and kept going past the outskirts of town until my folks felt like stopping. When Dad pulled the car off the road, we sprinted off in different directions—some to climb trees, some to catch critters, some to play hide-and-seek in the tall grasses, some to quietly explore foot-worn paths.

Those carefree escapades, some of my favorite childhood memories, seem like artifacts of another era. In a digital universe, unplugged spontaneity seems rarely sanctioned, if ever. It is sobering (to say the least) to consider that I am a part of a generation that has ushered in one of the most stunning paradigm shifts humanity has ever known.

I have lived in both worlds. My childhood days were untethered—no Internet, no smartphones, no persistent pinging of e-mails and texts, and no social media beyond our rotary dial phone. Television itself was a special event, served up sparingly and always fit for the entire family. My adult children, dubbed *digital natives*,[1] bridge the gap—I am the *before* and their children will be the *after*—the ones who will play out this saga of a change so capacious that we cannot find its edges, pulled along as we are by technology's relentless pace.

About 2,500 years ago a sage named Heraclitus offered the familiar maxim: The only thing that is constant is change. The aging Greek philosopher was alerting us that the only thing we can know with certainty will never change is that things are going to change. In hindsight, his wisdom seems understated, for surely in his wildest dreams Heraclitus could not have imagined the stunning rapidity with which the world to which you and I awaken each morning seems to be altering its course. As journalist Douglas Rushkoff suggests in his book *Present Shock*, "Change is no longer an event that happens, but a steady state of existence."[2]

The nagging sense that nothing about our lives is secure, that change is the new normal, is fueled by our ubiquitous presence online. Wherever we go and whatever we do, we are connected—from our cars to our bedrooms, from our desks to our coffee shops, from our churches to our kitchens. Amidst the ever-pinging text messages, the beeping backlog of e-mails, the plethora of posts, pokes, and pics on social media, as well as the expectation that we must be instantly available to everyone—friend or foe—who might contact us, we feel permanently tethered to our devices, as if they are some sort of technological umbilical cord connecting us to the universe.

I am not personally prone to panic attacks, but these days there are moments when I find myself out of sorts, almost as if I can't quite catch my breath. I don't think I'm alone in this. People of all ages seem terminally distracted, perpetually hurried, and often harried. It is rare for an answer to the question "how are you?" not to include the word *busy* and elicit some degree of angst. Collectively it feels as if we are losing something important in the name of progress, as if life itself is slipping through our fingers.

Yet if this is true, why do we not question the rhythms and patterns that govern our lives? What is it that makes us move mindlessly through our days, caught in the swift-moving current of a digital culture that waits for no one? Perhaps more importantly, what is all of this doing to the state of our souls? If the Spirit of God wanted to capture our undivided attention, what might he ever so gently whisper?

And could we hear him amidst the cacophony of cyber-static that surrounds us?

As someone who is passionate about spiritual formation, these questions have arrested my heart and mind. I have studied and read and prayed and pondered, and to be honest, it feels as if I've opened a Pandora's Box with contents worse than I expected. There's little question that dangers lurk in this digital sea in which we swim day in and day out, and while these have serious spiritual implications for Christ followers, the church seems largely silent on the issue. Instead, the voices of educators, neuroscientists, humanitarians, medical doctors, politicians, executives, psychologists, and social scientists alike resound in an increasingly loud chorus of caution concerning the long-term negative effects that technology may be having on culture and individuals, particularly those digital natives whose entire life experience has been one of a 24/7 connection.

## My Love-Hate Relationship with Technology

Saturday night, circa 1959. Baths finished and pajamas donned, my four siblings and I were curled up on the living room floor watching hopefully while dad fiddled with the foil-wrapped rabbit ears that sat atop our small television. We were the first family on the block to get a color TV, an event that imbued us with almost-instant celebrity status in the neighborhood. There wasn't much content to choose from in those days, but if we were lucky and the weather cooperated,

Ben Cartwright and his boys would soon appear astride their horses as the *Bonanza* theme thundered its clip-clop tune and the credits emerged from the midst of a fire burning to the edges of the screen.

Fast-forward almost three decades to 1987. That particularly difficult winter, my vocal cords had been damaged from back-to-back throat infections, and the doctor forbade me to speak for a month. As a mother of two boys, this was an excruciating dilemma—until a good friend hauled over their Apple II computer. Now I could communicate by typing on a keyboard and watching my words magically appear on the screen. We were all in awe. Never mind that the computer was a cumbersome eyesore, taking up half of my kitchen table, where I had to remain in case I needed to talk to my family members—who, I might add, were far more enamored of that technological wonder than sympathetic to my plight.

These stories date me as a *digital immigrant.* I share them because they frame my perspective in writing this book. I have watched the ushering in of the technological revolution firsthand, and if I sound unduly alarmist at times, this is probably why. But truth be told, I love technology and can as easily become fixated on the next best thing as anyone else. I work from a computer with two monitors, and I have a two-in-one for travel, an Internet media center, an e-reader, and a smartphone. I use many of them continually, even in my morning devotionals, where a variety of apps enhances my spiritual quests. I am keenly aware not only that our hyperconnectivity is not going away but that the future will be increasingly difficult to navigate without a hefty level of technological acumen. Be assured, then, that this book is not a plea to return to the past, nor will it champion an unplugged life.

Yet, at the same time, I am disturbed at the spiritual losses that seem to be piling up, not only for individuals and families, but for the church at large, as a result of our wholesale and uninformed immersion into this digital universe. God has imbued our souls with certain capacities that are essential for knowing him and making his presence known in the world—things like reflection and meditation, communion and compassion, contemplation and listening, awareness and even prayerfulness. These and others are at risk, in part because of the frenetic nature of our lives, but more importantly because of the impact technology is having on our brains. Simply put, the neurological activity between our ears, which is greatly affected by our digital habits, has a direct link to our formation into Christlikeness. I believe the time has come for us to grapple seriously with this.

> THE NEUROLOGICAL ACTIVITY BETWEEN OUR EARS, WHICH IS GREATLY AFFECTED BY OUR DIGITAL HABITS, HAS A DIRECT LINK TO OUR FORMATION INTO CHRISTLIKENESS.

## An Honest Assessment

Are there moments when you sense that your life is out of balance, that somewhere along the line you've lost control of how you manage your time and energy? Let me ask this another way: Can you say with confidence that technology is a servant to your needs rather than a silent taskmaster over you? Perhaps you've not really thought about it, but consider this: Do you ever

- go online to read or watch something or check social media, and end up spending an hour or more lost in hyperlinks, while feeling like you have nothing to show for it?
- feel compelled to check immediately when you hear a ping for a text, e-mail, or phone call, regardless of who you are with or what you are doing?
- sit down to read a book and find yourself impossibly distracted, or realize after five or ten minutes that you can't remember a thing you've just read?
- set aside a time for quiet prayer but feel so antsy you can't get anything out of it?
- ignore the people who are right there with you as you play games online or engage in social media?
- find yourself waking up in the morning already on overload, feeling as if you will never tie up all the loose ends in your life?

If you found yourself answering yes—as most probably would—you are living out some of the negative consequences of a hyperconnected life. But here's the thing: Have you ever taken the time or invested the energy to consider what impact this is having on your walk with God? Do you ever honestly assess how your engagement with technology may be forming (or malforming) you as a spiritual being? My desire is that this book will challenge you to do just that. But at the same time, and equally importantly, I want to show you that there is a way out—that you do not have to be an unwitting victim of digitization. The truth is that God has given us all we need to recapture the capacities we need for our souls' well-being and to bring spiritual balance to our lives.

How? Surprisingly, the answers begin with the exploding study of the human brain called neuroscience, which has not only discovered the ways that technology may be reshaping our brains, but also offers great hope for turning things around.

## This Is Your Brain on Technology

When I was in third grade, Miss Small—a stout, gray-haired, no-nonsense Sunday school teacher who showed up every week in the same charcoal suit and white silk blouse—stunned our entire class by cracking a raw egg into a glass of beer, soberly warning us that the egg represented our brains.

The lesson itself, if there was one to be had, was lost on us. We squirmed and snickered in awkward awe at that can of Pabst Blue Ribbon sitting there on a Sunday morning in our Southern Baptist church. Truth be told, there wasn't an eight-year-old among us who had ever been in such close proximity to a can of beer, much less breathed in its yeasty aroma as it bubbled and frothed its way to the top of the glass.

Turns out Alice Small may have been ahead of her time, at least in likening a brain to an egg. In the mid-1980s the Partnership for a Drug-Free America launched an ad campaign with a close-up video of an egg dropping into a frying pan, while a voice in the background uttered the well-known phrase "This is your brain on drugs. Any questions?"

Aside from the fact that the texture of a brain is more like a bowl of Jell-O than the contents of an eggshell, these examples rightfully allude to a more recent, astounding scientific discovery: Our brains have the property of *plasticity*. This means that rather than being hardwired in the womb, as was once assumed, our brains are always changing, even into adulthood, making constant adjustments over the course of our lives based on our everyday actions and experiences.

Here's a brief overview of how this works. Incredibly, your brain hosts 100 billion neurons (nerve cells), roughly as many as the number of stars in the Milky Way. Any single one of these neurons can have up to ten thousand thread-like branches, which continually send or receive signals from other neurons—a bit like friends talking on the telephone. Between these branches are minuscule spaces called synapses, which is where these signals—your thoughts, perceptions, and memories—shuttle along like race cars at speeds of up to 250 miles per hour. When you go to sleep at night, this activity continues as your brain sets about the task of pruning. Neurons grow new branches and lose old ones, and neural pathways may be strengthened, shrunk, created, or destroyed based on what you did during your waking hours.

All of this relates to an important principle regarding the brain's plasticity, reflected in the increasingly popular phrase "Cells that fire together, wire together." In short, the more you engage in any one thought process or behavior, the more regularly specific brain cells fire together, and thus the more deeply entrenched those supportive neural pathways become.[3] This is how you establish habits and form mental models that end up determining, in large part, your way of being in this world.

What are the spiritual implications of this? Our ever-increasing engagement with technology is deepening neural pathways that make it difficult to maintain practices that are essential for soul care. For example:

- Our habit of continually switching from one thing to another on our devices trains our brains to seek constant stimulation, and this makes it hard to spend focused time connecting with God.
- The way we skim when we are on the Internet trains our brains for shallow thinking, so we struggle to take in transcendent truths that reveal the profound beauty of Christ.
- Compulsive texting, playing video games, and engaging in social media train our brains to neglect the person in front of us, robbing us of the awareness we need to be salt and light or to love our neighbors as ourselves.

These are just a few of the ways that our hyperconnected lives may be imperiling our walk with God.

## Finding Our Way Out

I hope you can see here that the stakes are too high for us to ignore. Yet because our brains have this marvelous capacity to adapt, we have hope: We really can take control of technology and make it work to our advantage. In fact, if you were to peruse a score of the latest books on technology and the brain, you would discover recommendations for a number of activities that promise to do just that.

Most of these recommendations are based on secular research. Studies indicate, for example, that *reflection* contributes to a well-rounded mind and an ability to "thrive in a complex, ever-shifting new world." *Meditation* strengthens your brain and is a "stepping stone to becoming more compassionate, calm, and joyful." *Prayer* can lower your propensity to anger and increase empathy. *Contemplation* can actually cause your brain to grow.[4]

It is a stunning fact that these practices and others were all laid out in Scripture thousands of years ago. In this book, I offer fresh ways to engage with many of these ancient spiritual practices. They can help you become a better steward of your digital life as you rewire your brain. To that end, we will explore four categories of our spiritual journeys, each one symbolized by a component from a discipline called *lectio divina* ("sacred reading"), which I use as a metaphor to frame the conversation.[5] Here is a short synopsis of what you can expect:

- *Lectio*—to read. This section will examine why we struggle with focus and how our waning capacity to do so is affecting our ability to think deeply. It includes simple practices such as deep reading and memory enhancement that can help us regain clarity and improve our ability to concentrate.
- *Meditatio*—to meditate. This section looks at the various ways technology breeds distraction and, as a result, a shallow spirituality. It includes practices such as God-focused deep breathing and biblical meditation, designed to settle our minds and hearts and to enable us to deepen our grasp of God's ways, works, and Word.
- *Oratio*—to pray. Here I explore how we have unwittingly yielded control over our thoughts and behavior to others, as well as the deficits we face relationally as a result of digital idolatry. This section includes practices designed to restore personal balance and foster authentic community through greater consecration.
- *Contemplatio*—to contemplate. This section considers how we lack awareness of God and his heart, both in times alone and as we move about in the world, because of the pace we feel pressured to maintain. It includes practices that foster a vision of God's love that both infuses us and informs our way of being in the world.[6]

## A Final Caution

I read recently that the amount of time we spend online, whether via computers, tablets, or smartphones, is becoming so hazardous that we will one day look back with attitudes much like those reflected today toward smoking—distress at the price we have paid, indignation that no one warned us of its perils. At the risk of overstatement, I have to say that this is the reality that troubles me day and night and has driven me to write this book. I am convinced that if we don't wrestle with these issues now, we risk forfeiting our destinies and those of generations to come to the tyranny of technological urgency.

Yet, as much as I'd love for scores of people to read this book, I must caution you that reading alone will bring no lasting change to your spiritual life. If I've learned anything from my own journey and the variety of sources

> THE ONLY WAY TO EFFECTIVELY OVERRIDE UNHEALTHY PATTERNS OF BEHAVIOR IS TO ESTABLISH NEW HABITS OF LIFE.

I've consulted as I've written this book, it is that transformation comes not through what we know but through what we do with it—or, in other words, through the practices we keep. The only way to effectively override unhealthy patterns of behavior is to establish new habits of life.

To that end, I pray fervently that you will take the practices in each chapter seriously enough to engage in them with determination and diligence. If you do, I believe you will be refreshed and invigorated as your brain is rewired, and you will find the balance you need to live in this hyperconnected world. Over time, your spiritual journey will deepen as your life is transformed for the glory of our Lord and the joy of your own heart.

PART ONE

# LECTIO

*Lectio divina is the kind of reading that frustrates the urge to get through, to get anything, but instead places the reader in slow time, where all the moves are God's. A person doing sacred reading has to resolve to waste time, a terribly countercultural, counterproductive move in this media- and Web-saturated culture.*

**MARIA LICHTMANN,** *The Teacher's Way: Teaching and the Contemplative Life*

# CHAPTER 02

# SLOW READING AND DEEP THINKING

*Thoughtlessness is an uncanny visitor who comes and goes everywhere in today's world. For nowadays we take in everything in the quickest and cheapest way, only to forget it just as quickly, instantly.*

**MARTIN HEIDEGGER,** *Discourse on Thinking*

READING, FOR ME, has always been a spiritual experience. There is something mystical, almost magical, about the manner in which random black marks form letters that coalesce to create words that have the power to alter the fabric of my existence. Whether principles to live by, proverbs for inspiration, or the promise of escape to some distant time and place, reading nourishes my soul.

I come by this naturally. My parents were readers. Bookshelves always filled at least one wall of our home, and family dinners elicited lively conversations about our latest endeavors. (I remember, for example, my sister chattering on about *The Catcher in the Rye*, her freshman English assignment, which prompted my father to peruse it himself, leading to vociferous objections in the principal's office.)

My own love affair with books came about almost by accident. In my formative years, our family made regular visits to the Goodwill, one of the many ways Mom managed to make ends meet on blue-collar wages with five kids. Not being particularly taken with the musty smells and racks of Middle America's detritus, I would curl up in a corner on the floor by the books, losing myself in glorious adventures and taking home treasures—*Gone with the Wind* or *Wuthering Heights* or *The Adventures of Huckleberry Finn*—that could be had for a nickel. My hours in grade school were tolerable only in anticipation of weekly library visits, and I am still a little awestruck every time I drop in at the local library less than a mile from my house, where a seemingly limitless supply of literary tomes awaits.

Of late, however, I find myself less inclined to pick up a book. And when I do, I am more easily distracted—I have to refocus often, perusing paragraphs two or three times, even starting back a few pages when I return the next day. Like most of the world, much of my reading over the past decade has moved from the printed page to online text, and in the process, it feels as if some sort of seismic shift has taken place. More often than I care to admit, I find myself preferring to watch television or surf the Web over reading a good book, and this troubles me. My relationship with print feels a bit fragile, as though it might be in danger of extinction. This is probably an overstatement, but I know I am not alone.

The simple truth is that, despite the fact that the Internet has made books—fiction and nonfiction alike—accessible in unprecedented ways, people are reading them less often than ever before. In fact, since 2003 when the government first started collecting data about how we spend our time, reading has steadily declined as a leisure activity. The most recent survey suggests that, while Americans over the age of seventy-five read slightly more than an hour on any given Saturday or Sunday, teenagers from age fifteen to nineteen read for an average of only four minutes. This same age group interacts with digital media for a minimum of ten hours per day. More than half of all eighteen- to twenty-four-year-olds report that they never pick up a book to read just for pleasure.[1]

A growing number of educators warn of the threats that our waning propensity to read holds, both for individuals and the culture at large. The resounding concern is what cognitive capacities we might be losing, not only as we read less but as we spend more and more time engaging with words on a screen rather than in print. For a variety of reasons that we will explore, many believe that the inevitable outcome of digitization is the loss of our ability to reflect and think deeply, with some going so far as to say that the Internet is making us stupid.[2] Maryanne Wolf, prominent scholar on the reading brain, notes that while it's too early to tell, given the nascent transition to digital reading, our brains seem to be rewiring as we move from print to screen, and we need to consider the impact of this as we look to the future.[3] Journalist Nicholas Carr concurs, noting that "for all that's been written about the Net, there's been little consideration of how, exactly, it's reprogramming us. The Net's intellectual ethic remains obscure."[4]

I am deeply concerned with even the remote possibility that, having transitioned to digital text, we may one day find ourselves unable to reflect or contemplate or ponder profound truths. These activities are essential to an authentic relationship with God and our formation as spiritual beings. More and more as I talk with people about these kinds of things, they nod knowingly, lamenting the mental deficiencies they already feel. Will times of quiet reflection in God's presence become a relic of another age? Will our steady digital diet generate a disregard for the inscrutable mysteries of God's Word? What kind of relationship will we have with the Almighty, whose thoughts transcend ours in every way, if we are unable to think deeply about things?

> WHAT KIND OF RELATIONSHIP WILL WE HAVE WITH THE ALMIGHTY, WHOSE THOUGHTS TRANSCEND OURS IN EVERY WAY, IF WE ARE UNABLE TO THINK DEEPLY ABOUT THINGS?

Equally disconcerting is what this might mean to the church at large. How will that "great cloud of witnesses" continue to influence and shape our thinking if we don't read their works? What will become of Christian classics such as those that were handed down to me as a young woman—*The Imitation of Christ* or Augustine's *Confessions*—or works that changed me as an adult, such as *Mere Christianity* or *The*

*Knowledge of the Holy* or *Celebration of Discipline*? Even given the ease of accessing them online, how many of us are going to be able to direct our focus long and deep enough to take in these kinds of timeless treasures?

My limited understanding of the reading brain, of how it is developed, and of the impact that technology is having on it has astounded and sobered me. I no longer take for granted the miracle of being able to make meaning from the written word and the reverberating influence this capacity has on every area of life and culture. I believe we owe it to ourselves to listen to what scholars and practitioners are saying about the hazards of forging blindly ahead on the wings of digital text—not only for our general well-being but for the health of our souls. This, then, is where we begin.

## The Reading Brain and Technology

Right now as you read this sentence, neurons related to several of your brain's processes—attention, memory, vision, auditory input, and language—are firing at such amazing speeds that you are taking in most words in as little as half a second. This seemingly automatic decoding of the text enables your brain to move within milliseconds to the next step, which is to make sense of what you are reading.

Comprehension is not a skill that human beings are born with; it is established in the circuitry of our brains over many years of practice. We learn how to pause and consider words, connect them with things we already know, or make

21

judgments or inferences about them in relationship to our lives and world. It is this part of the reading cycle—the one that trains our minds for in-depth thinking—that experts are concerned will fail to fully develop for digital natives or will be diminished for digital immigrants as the structure of our brains changes through technology.

There are a number of reasons for this. First, research regarding the way that people take in words on screens versus how they absorb print media indicates that these are two very different processes. While reading print is generally linear—back and forth from left to right as you move down the page—many studies measuring eye movements during digital reading show a sort of "F" pattern: Participants read across the top of the screen, skip down and in to the middle, and end up on the bottom left side. Even when we read our favorite book on the most sophisticated e-reader, something about the screen causes our brains to treat it like hypertext: scanning and looking for links, following this same pattern. As a result, careful perusal of the words themselves is often sacrificed to the god of speed that tends to dominate our digital worlds.

The second reason for concern, closely related to the first, is that numerous studies show that people are so distracted by the presence of hyperlinks, targeted ads or other digital interruptions, that they comprehend as little as 20 percent of a single page. While hypertext offers us unprecedented opportunities to expand our knowledge by clicking here and there, comprehension is something else altogether, gleaned over time as we wrestle with words and engage in the necessary tedium of thoughtful inquiry. Some educators suggest that we just need to train ourselves and our children differently so that we are more focused and intentional with on-screen reading, but many question how feasible this is. At least for now, the kind of reading that creates space for thoughtful reflection seems to be supplanted by scanning, as our brains are being rewired to quickly sort and store bits of information rather than engage in the more complex process of comprehension.

## A Call to Slow Things Down

Technology, by its very nature, privileges speed, efficiency, and immediacy. This, as well as the ensuing consequences, has created a backlash in many aspects of life across Western culture. One of the first to sound the alarm was Carlo Petrini, an Italian politician who participated in a protest against McDonald's and the industrialization of food as far back as 1986, a protest which birthed the *slow food* movement. Since then, everything from slow aging to slow fashion to slow parenting (and perhaps most recently, slow church) have sprung up.[5]

While the missions vary, each of these movements in some way expresses a discontent with the escalating costs of our hyper-existence and calls for us to take time to be more thoughtful about those things that are sustainable, whether it is human relationships or the earth's resources.[6] *Slow reading*, a philosophy that encourages a return to a more reflective approach to the written word, has joined the ranks of these loosely affiliated crusades. We can learn much from the slow reading movement, particularly as we consider our spiritual journeys and the impact that our reading (or lack thereof) might have on our relationship with God.

My husband, an avid reader, told me recently that when he really wants to get into a book, he no longer uses his e-reader. He came to this decision one day when he went to order an e-book that a friend had recommended, only to discover that it was already in his e-library; he'd purchased and read the entire thing less than a year before. Having bought his first e-reader a few years back, he had begun building an entire library there in light of its amazing convenience, not only for storing hundreds of volumes but for reading, highlighting, and transferring notes. He realized, however, that with the e-reader he tended to race along, taking in entire pages at a glance as he swiped away, which likely explains how he could have forgotten that recently read book.

But the biggest reason he was making the change was that he'd come to the conclusion that e-reading just wasn't as enjoyable as settling down with a printed book. Perhaps you can relate. Research consistently reveals that people of all ages find reading print media to be more satisfying and enjoyable than reading hypertext. This may be because of the pace that the printed word seems to foster. Books have a way of inviting us into their world like a welcoming friend who encourages us to take off our coat and stay awhile. Their structure calls for sitting with one page at a time, engaging in a thoughtful tempo and embracing a comfortable rhythm.

Think of the sheer physicality of a book—the way we hold it in our hands, turn its pages, fold down its corners, highlight key quotations, write in the margins, look back a few paragraphs, or read ahead should we feel like it. The book is present to us—it has a smell and a feel, its weight and size orienting us to how far we've come or what is in store. This tactile connection to a book animates our reflective capacities; it gives us an incentive to ponder. It helps us slow down.

## The Adventure of Slow Reading

When I first heard the term *slow reading*, I couldn't help but think of the iconic fable of the tortoise and the hare, with its implication that "slow and steady wins the race." Indeed, one book on slow reading has a picture of a turtle on the cover, while another carries that of a snail. Contrary to what one might assume, however, proponents of slow reading suggest that it is not primarily about speed or plodding through passages with dutiful determination. Instead, it is a practice that teaches us how to set our own pace, to discover for ourselves the best way to approach the text at hand. There may, for example, be times when we race through a page or two, only to have one word or phrase or paragraph suddenly grab our attention, bringing us to a hard stop.

Paying attention is the slow reader's bailiwick. Our goal, more than anything else, is to learn to be aware, to bring our full focus to the words we read. This means we work to hone the craft of *noticing*, and as we do, we will more than likely find ourselves slowing down. In a sense, we want to enter into a relationship with the text—listening not only to what is said, but also to what is implied and perhaps what is not said. We read, we reflect, and we organize our thoughts, relating them to situations we currently face or lessons we've previously learned. There is pleasure in this; it satisfies our souls. More than anything else, slow reading is an experience, an immersion into a "form of life lived at a higher pitch."[7]

Most of us can probably point to books that have elevated us in this way. As I was writing this chapter, Harper Lee, after decades of authorial silence, released *Go Set a Watchman*, her long-awaited sequel to *To Kill a Mockingbird*. I read this Pulitzer Prize–winning novel almost fifty years ago in freshman English under the tutelage of Mrs. Bloomberg, who challenged us to find one life-transforming lesson in the book and write a paper about it. I discovered mine in this advice that Atticus Finch gave his daughter:

> If you can learn a simple trick, Scout, you'll get
> along a lot better with all kinds of folks. You never
> really understand a person until you consider things
> from his point of view . . . until you climb into his
> skin and walk around in it.[8]

While I would be hard-pressed to tell you details of the story-line or characters from the book today, I've never forgotten that image of climbing into someone else's skin—it shaped me deeply, having reverberating effects even now. This is, perhaps, the greatest promise of slow reading—its power to change us.

## Strategies for Slow Reading

In his highly practical and helpful book *The Art of Slow Reading*, Thomas Newkirk writes of Asian religious traditions that identify something called "monkey mind." I love the image this phrase conjures up: a bunch of undisciplined thoughts jumping around in my brain like monkeys in their element, which happens a lot when I first sit down to peruse a book. Newkirk describes this as our "tendency of mind to be inconstant, capricious and unsettled."[9] Indeed. This is perhaps why one of the first things most advocates of slow reading address is the work we will have to do to quiet our monkey minds.

Reading slowly and deeply is a learned art—it doesn't come naturally, particularly to those of us whose hours in front of electronic screens have wired us for perpetual motion, our eyes ever darting about for some new stimuli. For this reason, we may have to invest time and energy, along with a strong determination not to give up, before we get to the place where the experience feels freeing and pleasurable. The good news, however, is that because our brains are malleable, they *will* respond. The more we practice slow reading, the stronger those neural pathways will become until we've established a habit that makes it almost second nature.

There are a number of books that explore slow reading

in depth, with most offering strategies and tips to enhance the experience. Some take a more literary approach that feels a bit like instructions for a college course, while others are simpler and more pragmatic. I offer a handful of ideas below that are culled from these, as well as my own experience. While they can work with fiction, they are more relevant for nonfiction texts. Because slow reading is a process of discovery, each of us must find what works best and then fine-tune it for our own needs. Perhaps these ideas will get you started.

*Consider the beginnings.* As an author, I can attest that we spend a lot of time trying to figure out what words to use to introduce the books we write. Thus, when you first open a book, take some time to read the beginning paragraphs a few times, perhaps even aloud. Reflect on what these tell you about the message you will be taking in or even the person who wrote it. After you've finished the book, take a few minutes to return to the beginning, looking at those words with the expanded perspective of the entire text.

*Interact with the text.* From the start, insist on being more than a passive recipient of the book's message. Instead, actively engage with it. Ask questions, consider hidden assumptions, and challenge thoughts by bringing in other perspectives. Pause to reflect regularly, or even set specific touch points for reflection, such as the end of every page or the end of each chapter. When you reflect, ask yourself questions:

- What am I being invited to understand here?
- Why does this stand out to me?

- What difference does this perspective make in how I live?
- Where have I seen this principle at work before?

*Read out loud.* Reading aloud creates a different experience with a text. It enables you to hear the words as well as see them, and this is helpful for developing your capacity to focus. When a paragraph or page either strikes you as interesting or confuses you with its verbiage, take some time to read it aloud, making your own decisions about when to pause and what to emphasize. You can even read it dramatically, trying out different voices and tones. When you do, you will not only comprehend more of the text; you may also feel a release of inner tension as you connect more emotionally with the text.

*Reread.* Take the time to go back and read passages that are particularly interesting or which require deeper thought to comprehend. When you read a passage a second or third time, look for new insights or try to find ideas you missed before. Be free with this practice: Reading something three or four times will not only help you to slow down but will also deepen your capacity to assimilate the text and integrate it with what you already know.

*Collect quotes.* Some authors are incredible wordsmiths, and reading their offerings can be like dining on a gourmet meal. Keep a journal nearby, and when you feel this way about something you've read, write the quote out completely before you continue on the reading journey. When you finish the book, go back and reread the quotes you've collected, or even return to them several weeks later. This is a great way to retain some key messages and is also excellent training for your brain in concentration and focus.

*Enjoy yourself.* The most important thing in slow reading is to enjoy yourself. Research has shown that the more we enjoy the reading process, the slower the pace we will take. If you find that reading feels overly laborious or you are simply struggling to concentrate, you might want to stop and take a few deep, slow breaths. This will relieve tension, which neuroscience has shown also helps our brains function better. As you are engaged in deep breathing, remind yourself of all that you have to gain, and then return to the text with fresh focus.

## Reading to Become Our Better Selves

The beauty of slow reading is that it enables us to rediscover what it means to be with ourselves, to connect with our own thoughts, feelings, and attitudes, away from the interruptions so pervasive to life in our digital universes. So rare are these moments that we can feel unsettled, as if we've been thrown into a room with some stranger who expects us to act like old friends. But as we press in, learning to sit within our own space by tuning out the distractions that fragment our capacity for reflection, we come to peace with solitude and find our inner worlds enriched. As we learn to attend to the words before us, we become better at attending to our own hearts, and in this, reading becomes a formative experience.

Surface skimming or gathering informational snippets seems banal in comparison to this kind of reading, where we learn to treasure each word, asking the text to help us transcend our narrow frames and alter our very understanding of the world in which we live. Thus, the interiority that is germane to slow reading does not constrict our souls but expands them, for it leads us into the realm of another's thoughts and dreams and hopes—to drink in new ideas and fresh perspectives, and to consider possible flaws in our own. This, C. S. Lewis suggests, is what makes a book good: when reading actually alters our consciousness, our understanding of how things are. "I see with a myriad eyes, but it is still I who see," the literary genius comments on the reading process. Slow reading is then, at its best, a venture that enables me first to know and then to transcend myself. What I will discover along the way is that "I am never more myself than when I do."[10]

## Why Slow Reading Matters Most to Me

On my bookshelf at home lies a tattered copy of Madame Guyon's spiritual autobiography, with the name "Naomi Harr" inscribed on the flyleaf. My Aunt Naomi, who has long since passed, began handing her books down to me when I was a young woman and just starting to grasp the mystery of a God who could be known. Madame Guyon's story captivated me from the start—this seventeenth-century French woman who defied the designs of culture and the dictums of the church to passionately serve Christ.

The presence of this book and a host of others by saints of old have, over the years, served to remind me of a subtle yet inestimable truth. Simply put, it is that my life as a believer is one moment in a continuum of time. I am a part of a grand narrative with a rich and varied history that includes the authors I read, as well as every person who has ever held their book in their hands. We, as the body of Christ across the centuries, share a collective story that has been passed down primarily through the printed word. And although I appreciate the convenience of having so many of these texts available online, when I read them there, they feel weightless, like disembodied limbs floating about.

Sven Birkerts, in his prophetic book *The Gutenberg Elegies*, predicted well before the Net became so central to our lives that the gradual move away from print media was having a deleterious effect on our ability to form a coherent worldview:

> Inundated by perspectives, by lateral vistas of
> information that stretch endlessly in every direction,
> we no longer accept the possibility of assembling a
> complete picture. Instead of carrying on the ancient
> project of philosophy—attempting to discover
> the "truth" of things—we direct our energies to
> managing information.[11]

The problem, it seems, lies with the medium itself. Hypertext by its very nature suggests impermanence. Its words appear and disappear; can be deleted, cut, and pasted; and made larger or smaller. Our unbounded exposure to digital media (along with the fact that our devices seem obsolete before we've even paid for them) suggests, perhaps on a subconscious level, that nothing lasts, that there is no eternal context within which to form our worldviews, no enduring spiritual reality to shape our faith. What might this mean for digital natives, well over half of whom today express uncertainty as to whether God even exists?[12] Lacking the context of a past, are these sojourners left to find answers within the nebulous now of their virtual worlds?

I hope that my children and grandchildren will one day hold in their hands books that I have treasured, and that as they do, they will experience a permanence and stability that transcends the technological universe that governs their lives. I want them to know what it feels like to be a part of something so much greater than themselves, to grasp the profound reality that they stand on the shoulders of millions of people of faith from centuries past, many of whom have charted their own spiritual journeys, theologies, and philosophies in print. Yet unless all of us—digital natives and immigrants alike—commit to reading slowly and thoughtfully once again, future generations may miss out on the beauty in the breadth and width and height and depth of our story—the faith-story of the ages. This alone is reason enough to embark on a journey of slow reading and deep thinking.

For wisdom will come into your heart,
     and knowledge will be pleasant to your soul;
discretion will watch over you,
     understanding will guard you.

PROVERBS 2:10-11

All this I have tested by wisdom. I said, "I will be wise," but it was far from me. That which has been is far off, and deep, very deep; who can find it out?

ECCLESIASTES 7:23-24

THE PURPOSE OF THIS PRACTICE is to experience slow reading. You will be interacting with short samples of two texts—one from Stephen Charnock, a seventeenth-century theologian, and the other from Dallas Willard, a twentieth-century philosopher and spiritual writer. You will be reading just two paragraphs, but your intention will be to focus on the content, to absorb the meaning, and to reflect on your own life in relation to what you have read for each segment.

## Prepare

Sit quietly in a comfortable position, with a pen in hand and a journal nearby. Take a few deep breaths and try to release the distractions of the day. With each inhalation, see God's peaceful presence filling you and spreading from the inside out. With each exhalation, see yourself releasing any burdens, concerns, or weights to God, who through his Spirit takes them and places them in safekeeping for this time.

## Read

The two paragraphs that follow are challenging and thought-provoking. Engage in the following steps *for each* paragraph, not moving to the second until you feel you have fully engaged with the first one. Try to be aware of the differences in the feel, the movement, and the content of the two pieces.

1. Read the paragraph very slowly, making sure that you don't skip any words, even small ones.

2. As you read it a second time, bring emotion to the words. You may want to read it aloud, as if you were presenting it to an audience. What phrases would you emphasize? What parts might you read loudly? Where could you whisper for effect? Where would you pause?

## Reflect

Read the paragraph a third time, asking yourself questions such as:

- What statement is this paragraph trying to make?
- What themes are represented here?
- What interesting revelation does this reading bring to me?
- What makes this relevant?

Jot down thoughts as they come to you.

## Respond

Spend a few minutes interacting with God's Spirit over what you have read. Share with him anything that has moved you, concerned you, or encouraged you. Ask the Spirit to guide you in this final question: *What one thing can be different in my day, my life, my relationships, and so on, based on an understanding of what I have read here?* Write down what you sense you are hearing.

## Reading One: Stephen Charnock, *The Existence and Attributes of God*

Whatsoever God is, he is infinitely so; he is infinite Wisdom, infinite Goodness, infinite Knowledge, infinite Power, infinite Spirit; infinitely distant from the weakness of creatures, infinitely mounted above the excellencies of creatures; as easy to be known that he is, as impossible to be comprehended what he is. Conceive of him as excellent, without any imperfection; great without quantity; perfect without quality, everywhere without place; understanding without ignorance; wise without reasoning; light without darkness; infinitely more excelling the beauty of all creatures, than the light in the sun, pure and unviolated, exceeds the splendor of the sun dispersed and divided through a cloudy and misty air: and when you have risen to the highest, conceive him yet infinitely above all you can conceive of spirit, and acknowledge the infirmity of your own minds. And whatsoever conception comes into your minds, say, This is not God; God is more than this: if I could conceive him, he were not God; for God is incomprehensibly above whatsoever I can say, whatsoever I can think and conceive of him.

## Reading Two: Dallas Willard, *Knowing Christ Today*

How are we to think about Jesus' presence today? No doubt volumes could be written on that question, and have been. But the simple fact is that Jesus Christ is present in this world, the only world we have, and in many ways. His teachings, even mangled and broken, have an incredible power to disrupt human systems, including the ones that claim to own him. He is the misfit and thus is available to all who would seek him. His crucifixion and resurrection announce the end of human systems and stand in judgment over them. He is the man on the cross calling us to join him there. He makes himself available to individuals who hear of him and seek him. In many forms both inside and outside the church, with its traditions, symbolisms, and literature, he is simply here among us. He is in his people, but he does not allow himself to be boxed in by them. He calls to us just being here in our midst. There is nothing like him. The people in the churches also have the option of finding him and following him into his kingdom, though that may rarely be what they are doing.

## Final Reflection

Before you leave this time of reading, consider what the experience was like. Did you find it hard to concentrate? Were you frustrated? Was it a peaceful time? What would you like to see happen in your life in relation to slow reading? You may want to set an intention for the coming week, such as replacing one session of web surfing with the slow reading of a particular text, or slow-reading a book using this format for fifteen minutes each night before bed.

# CHAPTER 03

# EAT THIS BOOK

*I want to hold out for traveling widely in Holy Scripture. For Scripture is the revelation of a world that is vast, far larger than the sin-stunted, self-constricted world that we construct for ourselves out of a garage-sale assemblage of texts.*

**EUGENE PETERSON,** *Eat This Book: A Conversation in the Art of Spiritual Reading*

MY HUSBAND AND I sat in the back row, new church planters eager for encouragement as we waited for the conference to begin. This was years ago, and while I don't remember the name of the event or even the speakers, I do vividly recall my first impression. "A Mighty Fortress Is Our God" boomed over the speakers as a group of somber men in suits filed silently onto the stage and waited, looking toward the back of the auditorium. Then, as if on cue, one stepped up to the podium and asked us all to stand in reverence for God's Word.

What happened next stunned me. Four men marched down the center aisle, each holding one corner of a black box on which rested the largest Bible I had ever seen. We all stood silently as they made their way to the front with great pomp and circumstance, placing the Bible and its box on a draped table. The conference had begun.

To be honest, the whole thing felt terribly unsettling. While I'm certain their intent was honorable—to instill in us a greater esteem for God's Word—the approach felt like overkill, bordering on bibliolatry. And yet it is this memory that I can't get out of my mind as I prepare to write on the challenges we face regarding our relationship with Scripture as inhabitants of a pressurized, hyperconnected world. Perhaps those conference planners experienced the weight I now feel, one that compels me to put the Bible on display in some way that will, at the very least, make someone sit up and take notice.

While I am aware of how easily my passion might be misconstrued, I cannot overstate the gravity of the threats I believe we face as a *people of the Word*. There are the statistics alone—while nine out of ten Americans own a Bible, with the average home having four or five, 64 percent of the Millennial generation (ages 18–29) do not view the Scriptures as sacred literature, and 39 percent say they will probably never read it. Far more troubling, however, is that of those who claim to believe the Bible *is* God's inspired Word, only 19 percent read it regularly (four or more times per week).

What motivates those who do find the time to read the Scriptures? The research here is also concerning. While just over half say they read to connect with God, this number is steadily decreasing. Instead, people are turning to Scripture more and more primarily for personal comfort or practical tips.[1]

What do these numbers mean, and how might they relate to our pervasive digital engagement? One answer can be culled from what people suggest as the primary reason they don't engage more with Scripture—they are just too busy.[2]

Something about this rings hollow: If efficiency is the holy grail of technology, then we ought to find ourselves with more time on our hands, not less. This past couple of days, for example, I have done a host of things that once would have taken me two or three times as long—from writing letters to paying bills, from locating information to purchasing groceries and gifts—all made easier and faster because of the Internet. Technology, however, exacts a paradoxical price: It offers us a vast array of ways to fill the time that it saves us. As a result, we feel constrained to take advantage of its largesse—surfing more, texting more, tweeting more, watching more, pinning more, e-mailing more, listening more, playing more, and posting more—as well as responding immediately to anything someone sends our way.

I live in idyllic San Diego, California, where ocean breezes blow and the sun shines most of the time. On those very rare occasions when we have really bad weather (and by this I mean more than one day of heavy rain), San Diegans get almost giddy. Why? Not only because we need it for our drought-prone environment but also because we finally have an excuse to slow down, stay inside, curl up with a book, or watch a movie—without feeling guilty that we're not going somewhere or doing something. Because our weather offers unlimited options almost 365 days a year, we who live here are prisoners of choice, ever obligated to make the most of what we've been given.

What the sun does to San Diegans is what the Internet does to all of us. By making itself available twenty-four hours a day, the World Wide Web compels you and me to take advantage of its endless opportunities until we can't imagine life any other way. To extricate ourselves on a regular basis seems impossible, even for something as central to our faith as engaging with God in quiet to read and reflect on his Word.

There is an even greater danger, which is that digital life can fool us into believing we are absorbing God's Word when our exposure is, in fact, negligible. For example, 81 percent of Christian Millennials posted Scripture on social media last year, with 13 percent saying they did so daily.[3] This is the sort of activity the Internet fosters. But how deeply do we engage with these short snippets that grab us with their fascinating fonts? Are we just gliding across the pages, picking and choosing and reposting without giving the text much thought? Is the extent of our theological reflection rooted in scriptural slogans or biblical tips from social media apps, YouTube videos, or websites?

Although it seems that any contact with God's Word would be profitable and surely preferable to no contact at all, we may be deceiving ourselves. A steady diet of decontextualized parts is risky, and it will certainly skew our understanding of who God is and of his overarching purpose for our lives and the world in which we live. Recently, when I encouraged a young woman to broaden her interaction with

Scripture, she explained that she really only likes to read passages to which she feels emotionally connected. Our failure to engage with the whole counsel of God's Word is our great loss, for God longs to share his entire story with us, to draw us to himself through a grand narrative that includes an incredible array of structures and forms—from loving missives to sober admonitions, from tedious histories to tender tales, and from intriguing mysteries to mundane genealogies.

## The Reading Brain and the Book of Life

The leading authority on the neuroscience of language, Stanislas Dehaene, notes that thanks to modern brain imaging, we now know that every time you or I read a single word in print, the combination of letters moves through our retinas and explodes into thousands of fragments within our brain, which then pieces them back together by asking a series of questions:

- *Are these letters?*
- *What do they look like?*
- *Are they a word?*
- *What does it sound like?*
- *How is it pronounced?*
- *What does it mean?*

As I noted in the last chapter, all of this happens in a millisecond without our awareness, an astounding feat that causes

Dehaene to ask, "How can a few black marks on white paper projected onto your retina evoke an entire universe?"[4]

Describing our propensity to read as a paradox, Dehaene points out that the human brain is simply like no other in its complexity and ability to learn. He estimates that recognizing isolated letters activates some five hundred *columns* of brain cells, and the number of neurons that fire when we combine letters into words and then string words together to make meaning is inestimable. Because only humans share these features of a literate brain, the neuroscientist concludes that it seems almost as if we have a "cerebral organ for reading."

Think of it: Not only did God choose to reveal himself through words, first spoken and then put into print, but he created you and me with this inimitable capacity to read them. Why? The most important reason is that we might know him—his ways, his character, his attributes, and his heart—not through the finiteness of an image set in wood or stone but through words that live, that are layered, nuanced, multiform in their power to illuminate, and yet always able to raise us to new vistas of revelation.

> THINK OF IT: NOT ONLY DID GOD CHOOSE TO REVEAL HIMSELF THROUGH WORDS, FIRST SPOKEN AND THEN PUT INTO PRINT, BUT HE CREATED YOU AND ME WITH THIS INIMITABLE CAPACITY TO READ THEM.

The marvel of the reading brain is perhaps matched only by the miraculous events that surround Scripture's history. While the Greeks invested the future of their culture in monuments that crumbled under the force of the elements, the Hebrews—wandering nomads more often than not—maintained theirs through holy words that accompanied them wherever they went. From Moses' transcription on tablets of stone, to the Jewish scribes' painstaking copying of the Torah scrolls on sheepskin, to the Greek codices of the early church inscribed on papyrus, God preserved his story. But this was just the beginning. For two thousand years this written record of God's interaction with humankind has been at the heart of a high drama involving corrupt kings and power-hungry religious leaders, devoted scholars and innovative inventors, and a host of saints throughout the centuries who simply would not give up on their dream of making the Bible available to every person in their own language.

The ease with which you and I can access Bibles today belies the tortuous road those precious words have traveled to make their way to our screens or shelves. With more than nine hundred different English translations and paraphrases available to us, it is hard to connect with the story of a young scholar named John Wycliffe risking his life to translate the first English version of the Scriptures as he painstakingly transcribed it by hand. The 140 million of us who have downloaded the most popular Bible app over the past few years[5] have probably never considered that we could do so only because men like John Hus and William Tyndale were once burned at the stake for propagating God's Word. Accustomed as we are to seeing the Bible top the bestseller list year after year with a hundred million Bibles sold or given away annually, we can't

even imagine Johannes Gutenberg's fifteenth-century print-
ing press with its first print run of just 180 Bibles.

An impressive 56 percent of Americans still say they believe
the Bible to be the actual or inspired Word of God without
error, which makes the fact that it is so rarely read all the more
a conundrum.[6] But we are a people who live in an age of perpetual motion, and we tend to wear our busyness as a badge of
honor. On those rare occasions when we do purpose to open
the Bible and read, we may well find ourselves hopelessly distracted. Philosopher and theologian David Wells suggests that
"the affliction of distraction" is the greatest challenge of our
age, and he goes on to ask, "How, then, can we receive from
Scripture the truth God has for us if we cannot focus long
enough, linger long enough, to receive that truth?"[7] Indeed.

## Confronting the Affliction of Distraction

In my daily devotional times I turn to my tablet to compare
Bible versions and check commentaries. I also rely on a Bible
app on my phone for memory work and word meanings.
These are amazing tools, and I am grateful to have them.
Yet when I want to read, ponder, meditate, and reflect on
Scripture in order to commune with God, I pick up my well-
worn print Bible. I made the switch back to it several months
ago when I realized that something about the digital experience felt sterile, like shaking hands with someone wearing
rubber gloves. The words are the same, and in fact more read-
able than my 1974 Broadman & Holman New American

Standard Bible, with its archaic *thee*s and *thou*s. But something about a hypertext encounter with Scripture makes me restless, and before I know it, I'll find myself checking e-mails or texts or even the weather. When I'm gazing at a screen, I find it hard to focus on God's presence, to listen to the Spirit, or even to ponder the beauty of the words before me.

I don't doubt that it's possible to engage deeply with God via digital media, but I suspect that our devices are much better at distracting us than drawing us into times of reflection. Recently, I had a conversation about this with a group of seminary students. Each one shared how he or she did not have any consistent rhythm of communing with God over his Word. While a couple of these future church leaders indicated a desire to do so, others appeared not to have thought much about the issue at all. There was an almost palpable sense of angst about their harried lives as the young men and women bantered back and forth. My heart ached for these overloaded students who couldn't even conceive of there being a better way.

The truth is that every Christ follower, by virtue of the Spirit who dwells within us, yearns for intimate communion with God. We are made for it. Prayerfully pressing into the Word that he has given us will not only transform our hearts and fulfill our souls but will also lead to more peaceful balance in all the parts of our lives. We cannot hope to live out our destiny as those called to *know God* any other way, but until we are convinced of this, we won't forge ahead with the discipline and determination needed to change deeply ingrained life patterns. Wells so very powerfully reminds us of this:

If we are convinced that we need, above all, to know God, to know who he is in his character, that will trump every competing interest. But we have to be utterly convinced. Being halfhearted and divided in our focus will not get us where we want to be. . . . Without this ability to stop, to focus, to linger, to reflect, to analyze, and to evaluate, we begin to lose touch with the God who has called us to know him.[8]

This ability of which Wells speaks—to stop, linger, focus, reflect, and so on, in order to know God—may be harder to come by than it's ever been. Because we're becoming increasingly wired for activity and motion, establishing the necessary neural pathways in our brains will take intention, follow-through, and some unique ways of connecting with God through Scripture.

Two of these ways—one conceptual and one practical—can be particularly helpful here, not only in helping us find focused time with God in his Word but also in establishing this as a life practice. The first is *receptive* reading, which strengthens our ability to focus. The second is *retentive* reading, which enhances our capacity for attentiveness.

## Strengthening Focus through Receptive Reading

Francis Bacon, known as the father of the scientific method, once wrote about the reading process: "Some books are to be tasted, others to be swallowed, and some few to be chewed and digested." Being a religious man, Bacon was probably hearkening back to times when the metaphor of eating a book shows up in Scripture. For example, the prophet Jeremiah offered these beautiful thoughts about ingesting God's message:

> Your words were found, and I ate them,
>     and your words became to me a joy
>     and the delight of my heart,
> for I am called by your name,
>     O LORD, God of hosts.

JEREMIAH 15:16

*Bibliophagy*, a real word that is used to describe the metaphor of eating books, depicts an earthy engagement with the words we read that is almost palpable in its effect. Eugene Peterson, author of *The Message*, wrote a challenging little treatise on this process, appropriately titled *Eat This Book*, in which he points out that often our approach to Scripture is to use it for our own purposes—knowledge or inspiration or direction. He exhorts us instead to "eat" it for God's purposes—to metabolize it so that it changes us:

> Christian reading is participatory reading, receiving
> the words in such a way that they become interior
> to our lives, the rhythms and images becoming
> practices of prayer, acts of obedience, ways of love.[9]

I refer to this kind of engagement with God in Scripture as *receptive reading*—we actively consume his Word by asking questions, probing ideas and pondering our own lives until it seeps down into the very bones and marrow of our being. To *receive* God's Word—whether reading a verse or two or an entire chapter—means to be thoughtful, disciplined, and deliberative about what we read, which requires a level of focus that may at first be difficult to maintain. But a consistent practice of even ten minutes a day can go a long way toward rewiring our brains for reflection and depth, making it easier for us to increase the time as our desire grows.

David Wells notes that there are three components to every communication—the words used, what the speaker hopes to convey, and the outcome the speaker desires in those who hear—all of which come into play in our interaction with God's Word.[10] I have summarized these with three questions that can help us secure and maintain our focus as we read:

- What does this passage actually tell me (the information in, or content of, the words)?
- What is God seeking to reveal about his heart, his character, his ways, or the motivation behind his words?
- Based on the first two questions, what response from me does this passage call for? (What is God's desire for me as I read?)

Whatever the methods we use to focus our minds and hearts on Scripture, we can never forget the wonder that the voice speaking these words to us is that of God himself. Because this is so important and so easy to forget, I always begin my personal focus in God's Word by acknowledging his presence in prayer, affirming my awareness that I hold his *living* Word in my hands. This prepares my heart to *eat* the words, to embrace the kind of receptive reading that honors the author and moves my soul.

## Strengthening Attentiveness through Retentive Reading

Augustine of Hippo, one of the greatest theologians in church history, was a lover of Scripture, perhaps in part because of his dramatic conversion when he heard a childlike voice singing, "Take up and read, take up and read," which he interpreted as a divine command to peruse the Bible. When he did, a light flooded his soul and the words from Romans 13 pierced his heart. For the next four decades, he displayed an unparalleled passion to know, understand, teach, write about, and live God's Word. While much of what he penned was theological and scholarly, the following offers insight into how practical his approach was.

> Whenever you read a book and come across any
> wonderful phrases which you feel stir or delight
> your soul, don't merely trust the power of your own
> intelligence, but force yourself to *learn them by heart*
> and make them familiar by meditating on them,
> so that whenever an urgent case of affliction arises,
> you'll have the remedy ready as if it were *written*

*on your mind.* When you come to any passages
that seem to you useful, make a firm mark against
them, which may serve as *lime in your memory,* less
otherwise they might fly away.[11]

Memorization of any kind, but of Scripture in particular, is
both spiritually valuable and incredibly beneficial for your
mind. Storing memories is something the brain handles in a
unique way. Because it cannot retain all of the things we see,
learn, or experience, neural pathways develop based on either
the emotional strength of the input—such as any traumatic
experience—or how much attention we pay to something
through concentration and repetition. Attention is like a
muscle in the brain: When we memorize something, we are
giving our ability to pay attention a workout, which in turn
strengthens and hones all of our cognitive capacities.

> WHEN WE MEMORIZE SOMETHING, WE ARE GIVING OUR ABILITY TO PAY ATTENTION A WORKOUT, WHICH IN TURN STRENGTHENS AND HONES ALL OF OUR COGNITIVE CAPACITIES.

This is especially important
as we grow older and the neural
pathways in our brains begin
to atrophy, causing memory loss and senility. Neuroscientist
Anthony Newberg likens this to a car that starts wearing out,
with various and sundry parts going bad a little at a time. Any
memory-enhancing program, Newberg says, will improve a
host of qualities—coordination, attention span, information
processing, problem solving, social decision-making skills,

even our intelligence itself.[12] Beyond that, memorization modifies our brains in such a way that the more we engage in it, the easier it becomes to learn and memorize even more.

When we memorize a passage of text, we internalize the words so that they become part of our makeup and our way of being in the world. Thus, when we commit things to memory, we are choosing to pay attention to those things that really matter; we are making an investment in the shaping of our personal worldviews. Yet, as important as this is, memory is becoming a rare commodity in this age of exponential knowledge growth.

## Outsourcing Our Memory

More and more we rely on a store of information outside of ourselves. Google founders Larry Page and Sergey Brin have gone so far as to indicate that their ultimate goal is a chip that can be implanted in our brains so we can have immediate access to the already more than 18 billion facts in their Knowledge Graph.[13] While it is incredible to have so much information ever at our fingertips, the way cells wire together in our brains means that the more we turn to external resources instead of tapping into our own memory banks, the less capacity for retention we will have.

Not too many years back, when I needed a Bible reference, I would search my memory. If I couldn't place the reference from memory, I would look up key words in a Bible concordance and peruse the list until I found the verse I wanted. Now all I have to do is ask my smartphone or begin to type a question in the URL field on my search engine—such as "what Bible verse talks about reaping?"—and I can instantly read Galatians 6:7 and related verses on scores of websites in any number of translations. While I could discipline myself not to use these tools, the truth is that I, like everyone else, find the convenience irresistible.

Although some argue that the face of knowledge has changed, that what we really need are new skills to retrieve and organize it, we are nevertheless spiritual beings. Therefore, accessing God's Word on our devices, no matter how quickly or easily, can never replace having it hidden in our hearts. This is why I've become far more intentional about committing Scripture to memory. But first I had to overcome a strong personal aversion to the idea.

When I was a precocious elementary school child, my pastor signed me up for a Scripture-memory contest. He gave me one hundred Bible-verse cards to learn in preparation for the event, which was less than one month away. I know I labored hard over them, but to be honest, I don't remember much beyond the dreadful contest itself. I sat there in the audience, palms sweating and heart pounding as if it would jump out of my chest as I tried to review those cards. They were beginning to look like some foreign language. Nevertheless, when my name was called along with that of a boy from some other congregation, I marched bravely forward. The two of us faced all those eager, expectant parents. The moderator began by giving me a reference to cite.

My mind drew a complete blank. The moderator offered

the same reference to my competitor, who rattled the verse off like clockwork. Then I was offered a second reference, and a third, and a fourth, all of which drew blank stares from me. I'm not sure how long this agony lasted, but at some point I began to cry. My mom mercifully escorted me back to my seat.

Needless to say, I have never been a fan of that kind of rote memorization, although it has its own benefits, I'm sure. Yet retaining God's Word is not only a valuable asset in our spiritual journeys, but it also uniquely contributes to the formation of our souls.

## When God's Word Dwells in Us

How often have you been deeply moved by Scripture in a morning quiet time, only to realize later that you cannot even remember what it was you read? The reality is that our brains are able to hold things in short-term memory for only about ten to twenty seconds. While study and meditation can help move God's Word from short-term to long-term memory, it cannot accomplish this as well as the concentration and repetition that memorization requires. Therefore, if we want to go through our days with Scripture moving, guiding, and shaping us, we will need to commit it to memory.

This, then, is *retentive reading*. Far more than an approach to memorizing verses, however, it is a lifestyle of committing God's Word to heart in substantial enough portions that it informs our way of thinking and being in the world. Jesus told his disciples that his words needed to *abide* in them (John 15:7-8), a sentiment Paul echoed to the church at Colossae: "Let the word of Christ *dwell* in you richly" (Colossians 3:16, emphasis added). What would it look like for Scripture to *live* in you, to remain *present* to you at all times? While smartphones have made it incredibly easy to carry our Bibles *with* us, committing Scripture to heart ensures God's Word is always at work *within* us. Even when we aren't consciously focusing on specific verses, the neural pathways we have created through memorization continue to produce reverberating effects.

We tend to memorize those things—such as oaths, pledges, or vows—for which we believe the language is so important that we have to know the words verbatim. Committing these things to heart, Thomas Newkirk notes, is "an act of loyalty and deep respect, of affiliation."[14] Memorizing Scripture is all of this and more, a tribute to the God who generously reveals himself to us through the gift of language, for it demonstrates that we care deeply about the things he has said. We value them enough to commit them to memory.

Dallas Willard said that if he had to choose between all the disciplines of the spiritual life, Bible memorization would be first. He called it "absolutely fundamental to spiritual formation . . . because it is a fundamental way of filling our minds with what it needs."[15] The formation of our souls is God's intent when he instructs us to store up his Word in our hearts, assuring us that this will help us avoid sin, live purely, keep from stumbling, and find delight in doing his will. He invites us to bind his words on our heart, promising that they will guide us, plant our faith in deep-rooted soil, and nourish our souls like food does the body.[16]

When we commit something to memory for long enough and with enough repetition, we retain it for life. This is why you know your country's pledge of allegiance even when you haven't recited it for years. When I visited my grandmother in a rest home in her final months, she didn't always recognize me, but her prayers were filled with Scriptures she'd learned long ago about God's goodness and faithfulness. Memorizing Scripture is like money in the bank, a spiritual investment we know we will be able to draw upon a day or a month or a decade later, even to our final days of life.

## Getting Practical

Earlier I defined retentive reading as a lifestyle of committing God's Word to heart *in substantial enough portions* that it informs our way of thinking and being. By substantial portions, I mean having a goal of several verses, or a chapter, or

> MEMORIZING SCRIPTURE IS LIKE MONEY IN THE BANK, A SPIRITUAL INVESTMENT WE KNOW WE WILL BE ABLE TO DRAW UPON A DAY OR A MONTH OR A DECADE LATER, EVEN TO OUR FINAL DAYS OF LIFE.

even an entire book. This was once a normal practice among Christians, and I am convinced that anyone can do it with a little time, discipline, and focused attention.

I have tried a variety of methods through the years—from secular speed-memory plans to online programs to Bible-verse memory apps—but the one I've found most helpful and enduring is Andrew Davis's *An Approach to Extended Memorization of Scripture.* He offers a number of excellent reasons for memorizing chapters and even entire books, such as having the overall context and understanding the big picture. My own motivation is that I've learned from experience that it is easier and more rewarding to learn a series of verses that flow together with a coherence and beauty only God could achieve than it is to piece together random verses like that Scripture memory contest of my childhood.

Davis points out that the Bible was originally penned for a largely illiterate culture whose exposure to Scripture was oral. Thus, when God instructed the people to meditate on his law day and night, he was telling them to commit the words they heard to heart so that they could focus on them during the daily grind of life and not just when exposed to religious events. For me, this means being able to walk through the passage or meditate on it while waiting at red lights or sitting in a doctor's office or as my head hits the pillow each night. While today we are blessed with the benefit of literacy as well as instantaneous access to the Bible, I believe we will gain far more as we internalize God's Word in the same way our spiritual ancestors did—by committing it to heart.

## A Return to Simplicity

I learned about Andrew Davis's Scripture-memory approach from a blog I regularly peruse, which brings me full circle here regarding the reading brain, technology, and our souls. Recently, my church joined an online Christian-media library that gives members of all ages access to an incredible array of Bible study and Christian-growth materials in every possible format: audio, video, printables, and online groups. Think of it—the finest teachers, the most popular studies, and cutting-edge media at our fingertips, any hour of the day or night! I can't even imagine how beneficial this must be to churches large or small and to believers all over the globe. Yet to be honest, when I visit the site I feel a little like I've just been dropped into the middle of a grand amusement park. Turning this way and that, everything seems so enticing that I end up hopscotching around, reading a snippet here, watching a minute or two there, trying to settle on one amazing lesson over the other. Perhaps you can relate.

There is no question that our digital worlds offer us incredible ways to enhance our spiritual lives, and for this I am grateful. I believe that all of us ought to take advantage of anything that might improve our piety and form us as Christ followers. At the same time, it seems that perhaps we need to step back every now and then and consider how we are really spending our time and what contribution our spiritual activity online is really making to our relationship with God. The danger is that we can spend so much time nibbling around the edges of all the choices out there that we end up feeling spiritually sated while never having communed with God in meaningful ways through his Word.

In times like these, it behooves us to remember that as

wonderful as it is to be able to access so many materials and options for growing in Christ, the most important resource we will ever have is the plain, unadorned Word of God. There is a blessed simplicity in sitting quietly before our Maker with only our Bible open in our laps. We read, we listen, and he speaks. Nothing else is really quite like it.

The law of the LORD is perfect,
  reviving the soul;
the testimony of the LORD is sure,
  making wise the simple;
the precepts of the LORD are right,
  rejoicing the heart;
the commandment of the LORD is pure,
  enlightening the eyes;
the fear of the LORD is clean,
  enduring forever;
the rules of the LORD are true,
  and righteous altogether.
More to be desired are they than gold,
  even much fine gold;
sweeter also than honey
  and drippings of the honeycomb.
Moreover, by them is your servant warned;
  in keeping them there is great reward.

PSALM 19:7-11

THE PURPOSE OF THIS PRACTICE is to experience God's presence through his Word by giving prayerful focus to a biblical text. Choose a passage of at least ten verses from Scripture ahead of time, and bring a journal to take notes. (Some recommendations for this kind of reading might be Joshua 1:1-10; 1 Chronicles 28:1-10; Matthew 9:27-38; Romans 14:1-12).

### Prepare

Begin by acknowledging two things in prayer:

1. God is present with you to reveal his heart.
2. God is inviting you to read this passage in this moment; it has been provided for your growth in grace.

Give thanks and ask the Holy Spirit to guide you and speak to you through this time. Work on your ability to *focus* on the text and what you are gleaning from it. If your mind wanders, simply come back to the Scriptures and to God's presence with you.

### Read

Read through the passage slowly and thoughtfully at least two times, bringing all of your attention to it.

## Reflect

In order to reflect on the passage, you will consider the three questions posed earlier in the chapter and expanded on below. Take the time to be thoughtful and prayerful, remembering that you are not interacting with words but with God himself. (Depending on the passage, you may find you need to break it up into sections. If so, work through the questions below for each part.)

1. What do the words say? What information do they provide? What are the facts here? Be sure to look for unusual details or things you might normally have missed. Don't move on to the next question until you feel you have fully mined the passage for all the information it provides.

2. What do these words tell me about God, the author? What do I learn of his character, his ways, his attributes, or his heart from this passage? What might have been his motives for including this in Scripture? Jot down what you initially see, and then go back and ask God to show you anything you might have missed. Ponder these things deeply.

3. Based on what I have seen, what is God's intention behind the words here? First, consider what he desired from/for the audience he was addressing when the passage was first written. Then prayerfully ask for personal revelation: *God, what is your*

*intention for me as I read this passage? Why have you invited me to consider this today? Is there a behavior to change? An action to implement? An attitude to embrace?*

When you have finished, write a brief summary of your experience, including an affirmation regarding how you plan to apply these things as you move through the next day.

# Retentive Reading

Heaven and earth will pass away, but my words will not pass away.

MATTHEW 24:35

As we have seen, memorizing Scripture is greatly beneficial to both our minds and our hearts. The purpose of this exercise is to cultivate *attentiveness* through concentration and repetition of Scripture. This practice will include the steps recommended in Andrew Davis's *An Approach to Extended Memorization of Scripture*. (This is an abbreviated version of only one chapter of his book. For further helps and an expanded understanding of the process, please refer to that book.)

This practice takes place not in one sitting but over a period of time, with an estimate of about one month. At first you will need only a few minutes each session, but over time that will grow. By the end of the month, you will need fifteen to twenty minutes at a time.

I have chosen Psalm 145 because it is an incredible litany of God's attributes and can become an invaluable part of your prayer life.

## Session One

- Read Psalm 145 all the way through so you have a context of what you will be memorizing.
- Read verse *1* aloud ten times, focusing on the words on the page as if you were taking a mental picture.
- Recite verse *1* aloud ten times, glancing at it only if you get stuck.

## Session Two

- Recite verse *1* ten times. (Review it first if you need to.)

- Read verse *2* aloud ten times, focusing on the words and taking a mental picture.
- Recite verse *2* aloud ten times.

## Session Three

- Recite verse *2* ten times. (Review if you need to.)
- Recite verses 1 and 2 in order.
- Read verse *3* ten times aloud as before, focusing on the words as they appear on the page or screen.
- Recite verse *3* aloud ten times.

## Session Four

- Recite verse *3* ten times.
- Recite verses 1 through 3 in order.
- Read verse *4* ten times aloud as before, focusing on the words as they appear on the page or screen.
- Recite verse *4* aloud ten times.

## Sessions Five through Twenty-One

Repeat the above process as outlined below. (You can see that it will take a bit longer each time.)

- Recite the verse you memorized in the preceding session, ten times.
- Recite the entire portion that you have memorized up through this verse.

- Read the next verse aloud ten times, focusing on the words as they appear on the page or onscreen.
- Recite this verse ten times.

If you work at this on a daily basis (even skipping one day a week), you will have memorized an entire chapter of the Bible in less than a month! To keep it in your memory, Dr. Smith recommends you recite the entire thing daily for another one hundred days. I find it helpful to practice reciting at other times throughout the day when I think of it. The more you speak the verses, the deeper those neural pathways grow. And because your brain likes the process, you will find you want to memorize more—it can even be addicting!

PART TWO

# MEDITATIO

*The inner meditative journey is not a weekend excursion to a land of sun and happiness. It is a way of life for people who actually feel a need for it and who have become conscious of their need.*

**MORTON KELSEY,** *The Other Side of Silence: A Guide to Christian Meditation*

# CHAPTER 04

# MAY I HAVE YOUR ATTENTION, PLEASE?

*We can create a culture of attention, recover the ability*
*to pause, focus, connect, judge and enter deeply into a*
*relationship or an idea, or we can slip into numb days of*
*easy diffusion and detachment. . . . The choice is ours.*

**MAGGIE JACKSON,** *Distracted: The Erosion of Attention and the Coming Dark Age*

ONE TYPICAL SUNNY SAN DIEGO MORNING, I was happily heading to the library to return two books and check out four others I'd placed on hold. This is a library I am intimately acquainted with and have used for years. Yet this time, for some reason, instead of taking the books inside, I dropped them in the slot by the front door.

The thing is, my library has no slot for books by the front door. I realized too late that I had tossed them in the trash.

After enlisting the assistance of the maintenance man—he had to use a special tool to open the large concrete and steel contraption—I sheepishly went on my way.

I, like everyone else I know, am almost perpetually distracted. What is worse, I seem compelled to feed this dragon. Why else would I be trying to write this chapter at a Starbucks, where indie vibes dance across the airwaves while a steady stream of people strain to hear overworked baristas herald their name and drink of choice? Why do I leave my e-mail open and phone on, pausing every few minutes to check for mail or messages? Why do I stop typing midsentence so often, gazing around the room and conjuring up imaginary life circumstances of some stranger who just walked in? And how in the world did I drink two cups of coffee and munch through an entire bag of almonds with no memory of having done so?

In the past couple of decades a cohort of educators, psychologists, and neuroscientists have sought to address questions like these and many others, dedicating themselves to the burgeoning body of *attention science*. Not only have they discovered that our ability to focus relies on a variety of networks in our brains, but this "cognitive tour de force," as *Boston Globe* columnist Maggie Jackson describes it, leads the orchestration of our minds, fostering the human species' "unique capacity to find meaning, engage in moral decision-making and even achieve happiness."[1] Indeed, it seems that our ability to pay attention is critical for the shaping

> THE ABILITY TO INTERACT WITH GOD THROUGH MEDITATION HAS ALWAYS REQUIRED FIRST FINDING A WAY TO DEAL WITH DISTRACTIONS FROM WITHOUT AND WITHIN.

of our very selves. It is of great concern, then, that by rewiring our neural circuitry, our pervasive digital engagement may be diminishing this essential capacity.

## Meditation and Attention

The ability to interact with God through meditation has always required first finding a way to deal with distractions from without and within. Yet it seems this need has escalated exponentially as of late. The refrain I hear again and again when I talk to people who try to engage in prayerful reflection of any sort is that they struggle with focus: Their minds wander, they feel anxious, and their brains are overloaded with things they need to do or plan for. As a result, many don't even try, or give up after a few frustrating days.

Meditation demands that we develop a single-minded kind of focus, to engage in what we might call *unitasking*. For example, philosophy professor Douglas Groothuis tells his students that the study of philosophy can't be distracted by tweets—"and if not philosophy, how much more should we aim to unitask our study of God and our prayer life?"[2] Perhaps this sort of unitasking is what Jesus means when he assures us that if our eye is healthy, our whole body will be full of light (Matthew 6:22). But how do we get there, and what would it look like if we weren't distracted?

Richard Foster suggests that there are three critical components to meditation, the first of which he labels *recollection*, which means "letting go of competing distractions until we are present 'where we are.'" Foster goes on to note that this will likely be something we will have to work at diligently in light of our disrupted lives.[3] But, as neuroscientists so often remind us, *what has been wired in can be wired out.* Because of the plasticity of our brains, we can have confidence that single-mindedness is attainable through patience and practice.

This, then, is the purpose of this chapter: to sort out how attentiveness works and to offer some ways that can help us let go of distractions so that we can be present to ourselves and thus to God, as well as to the specific focus of our time in meditation.

## Showing Up for Our Lives

Lately, I have been dealing with an uncomfortable reality about my cyberspace existence: Although the Internet has made an art form out of distraction, the only real power it has over my soul is that which I give it through the choices I make sitting in front of my computer or TV or tablet or smartphone screen, day in and day out. To be completely honest, I appreciate the Web's ever-present availability, the way it enables me to take flight as many times an hour as I want. What I tend to dismiss, though, is the trade-off—the destructive downside of too much digital engagement. It can keep me from showing up for my life, from being mindful of God, from living in the present moment, whether set aside for work, rest, connecting with others, or even play.

Cognitive neuroscientists would say that my persistent exodus from the moment at hand may well be a function of the part of my brain they call *bottom-up*, which refers to the unconscious system that quietly and continually operates in the background, taking in external stimuli and determining what is relevant long before it comes to my conscious awareness. The bottom-up system is involuntary and automatic, operating at the speed of milliseconds as it relies on intuition, reflexes, impulses, and habits. This is why I don't really have to think about things like brushing my teeth or tying my shoes. It also explains how I can end up across town and not remember anything about the drive itself. The bottom-up part of my brain handles these things on autopilot because they became routine long ago. Unfortunately, so did my cyber-life and pursuant propensity to flit from one thing to the other.

In contrast, when I am working at my computer and make any sort of conscious choice—for example, when I realize I've zoned out on social media and decide to get back to work—a very different part of my brain takes over. This *top-down* system, located in the prefrontal cortex, is slower and more meticulous. Often referred to as the executive function of the brain, this is what enables us to make critical decisions, to be self-aware, to reflect and plan and learn new things—in short, to *pay attention*. Because it cannot multitask, the top-down system switches back and forth when presented with more than one stimulus. It requires effort, focus, intentionality, and willpower. It can feel besieged by cognitive overload if given too many options.

In the interest of efficiency, our brains are designed to function as much as possible on autopilot, or bottom-up. When ideas or actions are repeated often enough, the conscious, executive function of our brains releases them to our more instinctual bottom-up system. It's almost as if the top-down system is determined to do its part well so that it can pass the job on to the bottom-up system, making room for new learning or more important things. So, for example, I have developed a routine of stopping every so often to save my work on the computer, and when I do, I take a few minutes to read e-mails, peruse social media, check the time, and look at my phone for messages. While this once required top-down awareness and decision-making, it is now automatic; my bottom-up system happily kicks into gear the minute I click on "file." I no longer give the process much thought at all. This is perhaps only one way that I've unwittingly yielded control of my time to the screen that sits before me.

For many people, a similar automatic routine is triggered by pings, beeps, or little red numbers on their smartphone or tablet apps. Regardless of where these folks may be or what they may be doing, when they hear that familiar noise, or the number catches their eye, they look to see what it is. Indeed, this habit has become so ingrained, and the neural pathways that support it so deeply entrenched, that some rely on it constantly. Everywhere we go—waiting in lines, sitting on buses, working out at the gym, eating in restaurants, listening in church, and so on—people are interacting with their tablets or smartphones. There are even apps that split the screen on our device so that we can see what's in front of us through our camera lens while we continue to check our messages.[4]

This explains, in part, why we struggle to focus in times of quiet with God: For us to stay present in the moment, to interact over truth with God's Spirit, our top-down systems have to secure and maintain control, which takes a level of discipline to which most of us aren't accustomed. As we have trained them, our bottom-up systems continually draw us away from where we are. The neural pathways that support a healthy balance between our top-down and bottom-up mental systems have atrophied, and we are wired instead for

> WE ARE WIRED . . . FOR CONTINUAL DISTRACTION. OUR ATTEMPTS TO FOCUS OFTEN FEEL LIKE ONE MORE BURDEN ON OUR ALREADY-TAXED MINDS.

continual distraction. Our attempts to focus often feel like one more burden on our already-taxed minds.

The simple reality is that if we want to be able to think deeply about God, to meditate on the truth of his nature or ways or words, and to encounter him through meditative prayer, we must regain our ability to concentrate—to *pay attention* as we come into his presence. Studies show that our minds wander an average of 47 percent of the time,[5] so this will take some effort. But cognitive neuroscientists note that even recognizing when this happens and deciding to return to the task at hand can alter the circuitry in our brains. In short, anything we do to train our minds to stay focused, for even short periods of time, will begin to turn things around.

## Finding Focus in the Quiet

Spiritual formation teacher Ruth Haley Barton likens her initial moments in solitude with God to an aircraft that lands hard on the runway, with the flight attendant asking people to remain in their seats until "Captain Crash and the crew have brought the aircraft to a screeching halt against the gate." Before Barton can even begin to connect with God's presence, she must clear away the wreckage of all her life distractions.[6] Evelyn Underhill, twentieth-century Christian mystic and prolific spirituality writer, agrees:

> The first quarter of an hour thus spent in attempted meditation will be, indeed, a time of warfare; which should at least convince you how unruly, how ill-educated is your attention, how miserably ineffective your will, how far away you are from the captaincy of your own soul.[7]

I relate to both of these, which is probably why I rely on a daily quiet-time ritual that serves, at least in part, to prime my body and mind to focus. Each morning after I've made my coffee, I sit in the same spot on the sofa in the same corner of my living room. A small basket holds everything I need. I take out my Bible and journal, turn on some soft music on my tablet, and grab a pen to jot down a brief list of yesterday's activities. So far, so good; because I've done this for years, my bottom-up system can handle it without me paying much attention at all. But when I try to begin my conversation with God—when I need my top-down system to take over—the wrestling begins.

In recent months I've established some simple focusing exercises to address this struggle. They not only serve to quiet my mind and body during my quiet time but also seem to have a residual calming effect as I go about my day. By engaging for a few minutes each morning in a combination of deep breathing, simple movement, and vocal sound (all while focusing on the presence of God), I've honed my ability to focus and learned how to more effectively connect with the moment at hand—and as a result, with God. I call this "God-focused deep breathing," or GDB. I will share more in the practice at the end of the chapter, but first—a little background on the science and context behind each of these components.

## Deep Breathing

There is a spirituality in slowing our bodies down to take in the air God provides. Yahweh breathed life into Adam's nostrils (Genesis 2:7); Christ breathed his Spirit into the disciples before his ascension (John 20:22). We are embodied creatures, sentient beings, and yet we tend to compartmentalize our relationship with God, forgetting that our piety encompasses body, soul, and spirit. Learning to breathe deeply is a way to remind ourselves of this. Not only does it calm our emotions as we inhale God's peace, but it enables us to recollect our minds as we exhale the distractions fluttering around in our brains.

The scientific evidence for the positive physiological effects of deep breathing is strong. We may not realize how shallow our breathing is most of the time, largely because of the stress of life. This reduces the amount of oxygen to our brains, hindering our ability to concentrate. Shallow breathing also causes a buildup of carbon dioxide in our systems, which can create anxiety and disorientation. Deep breathing is, therefore, a cleansing act, dispelling toxins and calming our parasympathetic nervous system. The physiological effects of this alone can be powerful—from lowering or stabilizing blood pressure to diminishing the symptoms of heart disease or asthma. Beyond that, deep breathing increases our mental alertness and cognitive processing.[8]

These recent scientific discoveries notwithstanding, deep breathing is not a new practice for Christian believers. For example, a thirteenth-century Eastern Orthodox monk named Nikiphoros wrote:

> Seat yourself, then, concentrate your intellect, and lead it into the respiratory passage through which your breath passes into your heart. Put pressure on your intellect and compel it to descend with your inhaled breath into your heart.[9]

In his ancient wisdom, Nikiphoros was encouraging us to use breath to concentrate on heart issues, promising that by uniting our intellect with our soul in this way, we would experience indescribable delight.

Ignatius of Loyola, the sixteenth-century founder of the Jesuits and author of *The Spiritual Exercises*, called one of his three kinds of prayer "prayer by rhythm." This included inhaling deeply, then speaking a word or two of a learned prayer while exhaling. "With each breath in or out, one has to pray mentally, saying one word of the OUR FATHER, or of another prayer which is being recited: so that only one word be said between one breath and another."[10] A twentieth-century Christian writer described this process as being "almost like communication with the less conscious parts of one's being, saying to them: 'Simmer down and listen, there is something beyond this turmoil.'"[11]

I have found deep breathing to be immensely helpful at the start of my time of meditation with God. Not only does it settle my soul and help me focus, but it reminds me of the fragility of life, of how my very existence depends on the will of God who gives to all life and breath and everything (Acts 17:25).

## Simple Movement

It is amazing that so much good can come from something as simple as tapping your fingers or palms together, or patting your right foot and then your left. These simple movements can improve your ability to think, lessen feelings of stress or anxiety, and improve your memory at the same time. How? As we learned earlier, our brain cells communicate with one another by sending signals across synapses to each other. Every neuron contains both a sending point, called an axon, and thousands of receivers, called dendrites, which are critical for optimal brain functioning. The daily stresses of life damage those dendrites, diminishing our brain's ability to process. Studies have shown that focused, repetitive movement can slow down dendrite deterioration, bringing healing to our brains and relieving us of feelings of stress, depression, or even anger. This explains in part why treatments that involve finger tapping have proved promising for everything from posttraumatic stress disorder to hypertension and fibromyalgia.[12]

Repetitive movement appears to engage a part of our brain's attention network called our "orienting" response, which is what enables us to sort through a variety of stimuli to determine what is important. Your orienting response enables you to listen to the person sitting with you at a crowded restaurant, rather than the orders a waiter is taking across the way. Anything we can do to hone this ability is a vital asset, for it enables us to more quickly tune into what really matters and ignore what doesn't. For many of us, our orienting response is in constant overdrive because of the bombardment of distractions that come our way on a continual basis. Repetitive movement has been shown to strengthen our orienting response. It makes sense, then, that it can help to hone our ability to listen for the gentle voice of God's Spirit as we go through our days.

## Vocal Sound

The final element in our focus triad is vocal sound, which hones our attention skills as we exhale sounds during our deep breathing. Although even silent repetition of a meaningful phrase can help us focus, a quiet voice gently speaking or singing a few words of Scripture, a prayer, or a hymn establishes a more consistent deep breathing pattern and improves cognition by engaging our auditory system. When we sing as we exhale, we intensify our emotional experience and soothe our nervous system while activating higher thinking centers in the brain.[13]

This is perhaps my favorite part of the focusing exercise. I have tried a variety of ways to bring sound into my God-focused deep breathing. Sometimes I sing the lines of a hymn, one at a time; other times I make up my own songs, using the Psalms or other Scriptures. There are times when I read lines of Scripture or use passages I've memorized, even well-known ones such as the Lord's Prayer (as Ignatius suggests) or Psalm 23. When I am speaking rather than singing, I like to play classical music in the background at a very low volume, which likewise has been shown to enhance cognitive functioning.

## Faith and a Few Minutes a Day

Dr. Andrew Newberg, perhaps the most respected neuroscientist studying the effect of spiritual practices on the brain, has used brain-imaging techniques to observe the brains of thousands of people—some from a variety of religious persuasions and others with no religious bent—as they engage in some combination of these three elements. These studies document positive changes in the neural circuitry of the participants, some of whom spend hours at a time engaging in the practice. Newberg suggests, however, that it only takes about twelve minutes a day to gain optimal benefits, with observable changes in our brain chemistry in as little as two months.

Newberg adds a fourth important aspect to God-focused deep breathing, which he calls "faith"—an interesting choice of words, given that he is a self-proclaimed agnostic. Specifically, Newberg encourages us that setting a goal for our focusing exercise, and believing that it will help us accomplish that goal, enhances the effectiveness of our practice.[14]

Personally, I can think of no greater goal than to bring all the powers of my attention to bear on my relationship with the One who created me to know him intimately. When I first began practicing God-focused deep breathing, it took me out of my comfort zone, but over time I recognized that it is a gift from God, a way to engage my whole being—body, soul, and spirit—so that I might move more quickly to a meaningful time alone with him. This is only one of the benefits, but for me it is the most powerful.

# GOD-FOCUSED DEEP BREATHING

ESTIMATED TIME: 12 MINUTES A DAY

But I have calmed and quieted my soul,
  like a weaned child with its mother;
  like a weaned child is my soul within me.

PSALM 131:2

May God himself, the God who makes everything
holy and whole, make you holy and whole, put you
together—spirit, soul, and body—and keep you fit
for the coming of our Master, Jesus Christ.

1 THESSALONIANS 5:23, MSG

In God-focused deep breathing (GDB) it is absolutely critical to use all of its components to help you concentrate on what you are doing. For example, when you inhale, you focus on your breath as you count silently, and when you exhale, you focus on the words you are speaking or singing, continually bringing your mind to the moment. The more comfortable you are with each part, the better you will be able to do this.

We will practice each one alone and then put them together, beginning with deep breathing.

## Deep Breathing

Your breath must be diaphragmatic, which means that your stomach visibly rises when you inhale and falls when you exhale (many people think expanding their chest is deep breathing, but it is not). For this practice, you will breathe in through your nose and out through your mouth.

Try a few deep breaths by placing your hands on your stomach to feel the movement. Inhale as you count slowly from one to five, about once per second. Then pause for a second, and exhale as you count from one to five again.

Once you've established a pattern of inhaling and exhaling from the diaphragm, move on to simple movement.

## Simple Movement

While any repetitive movement can work here, one of the simplest ways is to place your hands with palms together in a prayer pose, fingers touching. As you exhale, tap your fingers together one at a time, beginning with your thumbs. In the beginning, when your exhalations are shorter, you will probably only tap through the hand once. Over time, however, as you begin to inhale and exhale more deeply, you can repeat the movement as many times as necessary while exhaling.

Once you feel comfortable with this, move on to vocal sound.

## Vocal Sound

There is a vast variety of Scripture passages, hymns, or even self-composed songs you can use to give sound to your exhales. To begin, it is helpful to use something you are very familiar with so that you can close your eyes and relax through the process. To that end, we will start with the hymn "Amazing Grace."

Take in a deep breath, and as you exhale, quietly sing one line of the hymn. On your next exhale, sing the next line. If you find that a full line is too much, do half of the line instead.

Once you feel comfortable doing this, move on to the final step—putting it all together.

## Putting It All Together

Find a comfortable position in a quiet place and eliminate external distractions as much as possible. (Once you've mastered GDB, you will be able to engage in it anywhere you go, but first you need to become familiar through practice.) Place your hands together, palms open in a prayer pose, with both feet resting comfortably on the ground. Use the template below to begin.

- Inhale: Count slowly and silently to five as you take in a deep breath. Pause briefly.

- Exhale: As you slowly release the air, tap your fingers together while softly singing, "Amazing Grace, how sweet the sound."

- Inhale: Count slowly and silently to five as you take in a deep breath. Pause briefly.

- Exhale: As you slowly release the air, tap your fingers together and softly sing, "That saved a wretch like me."

- Inhale: Count slowly and silently to five as you take in a deep breath. Pause briefly.

- Exhale: As you slowly release the air, tap your fingers together and sing softly, "I once was lost but now am found."

- Inhale: Count slowly and silently to five as you take in a deep breath. Pause briefly.

- Exhale: As you slowly release the air, tap your fingers together while singing softly, "Was blind but now I see."

Continue this pattern through as many verses of the song as you can remember.

## Further Ideas

While the breathing remains the same for all GDB, you can change your simple movements and vocal sound. Experiment with different things and you will find what works best for you. The goal is to do this for about twelve minutes a day, but any amount of time will produce some benefits. Other movement ideas include the following:

- Engage in GDB while taking a walk, five steps inhaling and five steps exhaling.
- Lightly clap your hands or tap your feet during the exhalations.
- Fold your hands with fingers intertwined and gently squeeze them together several times as you exhale.

Other vocal sound ideas:

- Recite memorized verses of Scripture, breaking them down into parts to match your exhalations. (Psalm 145 works great.)

- Make a list of attributes of God and use one for each exhalation, giving silent thanks and worship as you do.
- Use the "Jesus Prayer" throughout GDB: "Lord Jesus Christ . . . Son of God . . . have mercy on me . . . a sinner."
- Recite the Lord's Prayer, using only a word or two for each exhalation: "Our Father . . . who art . . . in heaven . . ."

You can practice GDB when you are in a crowd, but instead of audible sound, sing or speak it in your mind. It's a great practice to engage in when you are driving, in order to connect with God, calm your nerves, and prepare you for a coming meeting or other activity. This is also a wonderful tool to use with children. They love to see how their stomachs move up and down, and the finger tapping keeps them engaged. Teachers who would like to increase their students' attentiveness can involve an entire class in GDB.

Be patient with yourself as you implement this practice. While you will experience immediate benefits, it won't become completely natural until you've engaged in it for some time. Try different approaches based on the three core elements—breath, movement, and sound—until you find what works best for you. Given the unrelenting pressure of the distractions that inundate most of us, we will have to be intentional, determined, and consistent, taking comfort in knowing that God's Spirit is working with us to change the very structure of our brains.

# CHAPTER 05

# MEDITATION—THE LABORATORY OF THE SOUL

*A meditative mind can be strangely reminiscent of how we experienced the world as a child. We're exquisitely ready for fresh illumination, hungry and wide open for novel insights, but at the same time, deliciously bathed in the present moment.*

**DANIEL BOR,** *The Ravenous Brain*

ONE OF MY TWO ADULT SONS is the family tech expert, the one we turn to when our hard drives crash or our Internet is on the blink or we can't figure out how to work an app on our smartphones. He is a true digital native, weaned on the family computer with the oversized monitor that loomed from a table in our dining room throughout his growing-up years.

When Jonathan was eight or nine, he became enthralled with a game that had something to do with theme parks. I never really understood how it worked, but somehow through the magic of programming he was able to design virtual amusement parks replete with rides, food stands, bushes, trees, and people moving along paths. I was particularly amused by the roller coasters that he worked on tirelessly; when done right, they produced tiny figures flying up and down the track in cars, screaming as carnival music played in the background.

As brilliant as my son's computational skills seemed, the philosopher Martin Heidegger would say that his game relied on *calculative thinking* rather than *meditative thinking*. In short, meditative thinking, a capacity unique to our species, looks for the meaning behind an event, experience, person, or thing; calculative thinking, meanwhile, focuses on what is useful. As my son constructed bigger and better roller coasters, he was concerned solely with which keystrokes would produce the effect he wanted. He probably never pondered why certain people are thrill-seekers, or what an amusement park's existence might reveal about the culture, or even what his own propensity to play the game for hours on end revealed about his soul.

While Heidegger wrote his *Discourse on Thinking* in 1959, long before the average person could even imagine having a home computer, his predictions about the rise of calculative thinking resonate with sober accuracy today. He observed then that people were becoming less and less interested in the meaning behind things. There in the infancy of the digital invasion, he was concerned that we would not be prepared to think deeply about the changes to come. Heidegger described this shift as more dangerous than the destructive potential of atomic energy and warned that "the approaching tide of technological revolution in the atomic age could so captivate, bewitch, dazzle, and beguile man that calculative thinking may someday come to be accepted and practiced as *the only way of thinking.*"[1]

Many would say we are on our way to fulfilling Heidegger's prophetic words. More and more we feel pressured to prioritize efficiency, multitasking ourselves into states of anxiety or exhaustion and rarely finding the space to really think about how we pass our time or what our relationship to technology might mean—to us as individuals and to our culture at large. There is no going back, we know. With the proverbial genie out of the bottle, our digital immersion will only increase in the years to come. So how are we to counteract this destructive inclination to blindly settle for what author Nicholas Carr calls "the shallows,"[2] where we master the art of managing information but fail to experience the joy of discovering truth—where knowledge is ever at our fingertips yet wisdom evades our grasp?

One proven means of counteracting these things is a practice rooted in our ancient history as people of faith: biblical meditation. Made in the image of God himself, our soul (encompassing our mind, will, and emotions) enables us to ponder life's most critical questions—and, in fact, find fulfillment in doing so. This is perhaps why God challenged the Hebrew people to be diligent about keeping their souls (Deuteronomy 4:9), or why King Solomon promised that finding wisdom and discretion would bring life to our souls (Proverbs 3:22).

Meditation is a powerful way to engage our souls with focused intentionality that produces numerous benefits, some of which the Bible has long touted and others of which science has more recently affirmed. But first, what is biblical meditation, and how does it differ from similar practices so popular in our culture today?

## The Uniqueness of Biblical Meditation

The term *meditation* is bandied about by a diverse army of proponents—from business executives to educators to talk show hosts to personal trainers—and the practices they promote are varied and nuanced. In general, however, most secular writing and teaching about meditation today refers to focusing and relaxation exercises (much like God-focused deep breathing, which I explored in the last chapter). Using some combination of breath and single-minded concentration, the emphasis is on calming the mind, but not necessarily stretching it.

While these practices are valuable on a number of levels and can be used to prepare our hearts for time with God, they do not fit the understanding of meditation that the Bible provides. There are two Hebrew words that are often translated as *meditation* in Scripture. The first, *hagah*, is an intriguing term used to describe everything from a lion growling over its prey to the sound of a harp being struck or a dove cooing. The idea is that of muttering or musing or talking to oneself in response to something. The other word, *siyach*, incorporates concepts such as bringing forth, musing, studying, and pondering.[3] Both words come together in Psalm

143:5: "I meditate [*hagah*] on all that you have done; I ponder [*siyach*] the work of your hands."

Most references to meditation in Scripture call for a focus on God's Word—his laws, statutes, and precepts. For example, as Joshua prepared to lead the people into the Promised Land, God told him, "This Book of the Law shall not depart from your mouth, but you shall meditate on it day and night" (Joshua 1:8). Similarly, the psalmist wrote, "I will meditate on your precepts and fix my eyes on your ways" (Psalm 119:15). Other topics identified for meditation in Scripture include God's works, his ways or attributes, and simply God himself.[4]

Every human being thinks about God at some point. Those thoughts begin to establish pathways in our brain, whether we cultivate actual faith or not. And the truth is, our brains are capable of such depth and breadth that it seems we can never be fully satisfied, no matter how much we study, learn, or meditate on spiritual realities. Indeed, as one neuroscientist notes, "The more one contemplates God, the more mysterious God becomes."[5] When I read this I couldn't help but think of God's reminder that his thoughts and ways are as far from ours as the heavens are from the earth (Isaiah 55:9); no one really comprehends God's thoughts except his Spirit (1 Corinthians 2:11). As Christ followers, we will simply never run out of material upon which to meditate.

> AS CHRIST FOLLOWERS, WE WILL SIMPLY NEVER RUN OUT OF MATERIAL UPON WHICH TO MEDITATE.

From the countless calls in the Old Testament to *remember* what God has done, to practical reminders in the New Testament epistles to *fix our minds* on complex issues like truth or loveliness or honor, God continually elevates the role of the human mind. From a biblical perspective, however, the mind is not limited to cognitive understanding. It encompasses everything from perceiving to feeling to judging to deciding. *Vine's Expository Dictionary* describes the mind as the "seat of reflective consciousness,"[6] which points to the very capacity that sets us apart from every other species—our consciousness, our ability to reflect or to be self-aware.

Thus, Christian meditation is much more than a mental exercise; it is "the laboratory of the soul,"[7] where God does some of his most important work in transforming us from the inside out. Richard Foster explains that meditation enables us to create "the emotional and spiritual space that allows God to construct an inner sanctuary in the heart."[8] I will end this chapter with ways to help us ensure this is taking place as we meditate, but first a look at the transformative benefits of this practice.

## The Astounding Benefits of Meditation

There are so many beautiful promises in Scripture related to meditation: It can satisfy our souls like a gourmet meal, make us successful on our spiritual pilgrimage, and keep our minds in a place of peace, to name a few.[9] From a scientific perspective, meditation literally changes the structures of our brains, making them healthier in every way. Because of their neuro-plasticity, whenever any human being ponders or muses on a deep truth or complex concepts, positive changes take place. But bringing God into the picture ups the ante. Here's how neuroscientist A. B. Newberg explains it:

> If you contemplate something as complex or mysterious as God, you're going to have incredible bursts of neural activity firing in different parts of your brain. New dendrites will rapidly grow and old associations will disconnect as new imaginative perspectives emerge.[10]

The bursts of neural activity between two of these brain parts in particular—the prefrontal cortex and the amygdala—are significant for our spiritual journeys and give us insight into why meditation is integral to our formation as Christ followers. Stay with me here, because what I am about to share is a powerful reality.

The prefrontal cortex is a hub of activity at the front part of our brains. As part of the top-down system, it serves a bit like the brain's air-traffic controller—directing thoughts and determining priorities so that we can function efficiently in the world. This gray matter above our eyes is what enables us to do things like make decisions, enjoy music, love our children, learn a new language, or think about God. It doesn't fully develop until around age twenty-five.

The almond-sized amygdala, located in the bottom-up

system, is often referred to as the brain's emotional center. In some ways, the amygdala can be like an unruly child, easily activated by circumstances and at the whim of a host of feelings, from joy to fear to despair. Because many more neural pathways run from the amygdala to the prefrontal cortex than the other way around, we often find ourselves operating more from how we feel than from what is right or rational.

Ideally, as we mature, the prefrontal cortex increasingly shapes and controls our emotions, communicating effectively with our amygdala to keep it in balance. But as you and I know from experience, this doesn't always happen. As much as we try to maintain control, our emotions often get the best of us.

This tendency has escalated because of the persistent demands of digital life. In our multitasking world, where we are bombarded by stimuli and under continual pressure to attend to multiple things at once, the prefrontal cortex is often overloaded—kind of like an air-traffic controller who has had no sleep and is trying to handle ten times the number of planes he or she trained for. As a result, we lose our ability to concentrate and effectively manage our mental life, a malady that most of us would probably say we face daily. There is an almost palpable sense that culture-wide we are characterized by frustration, stress, anxiety, anger, and even rage.

This is where meditation can have an astounding impact. When we take the time to put away distractions and ponder God's Word or works or ways, we strengthen the neural pathways from our prefrontal cortices to our amygdalas.

Over time this increases our capacity to focus so that we can more intentionally allow God's Spirit to direct our thoughts and control our emotions. This is why Scripture says we are transformed by the renewing of our minds (Romans 12:2). In essence, through meditation, we are aligning our brains with the work the Holy Spirit is doing in our hearts.

A host of brain-imaging studies done while people meditate has confirmed this benefit of strengthening neural pathways, as well as a plethora of other benefits. For example, deep thinking and quiet reflection can enhance our ability to empathize with others, make us more socially aware, reduce negative feelings, counter effects of depression, help achieve our goals, increase creativity and spatial processing, and give us fresh perspectives on the problems we face, all while reducing stress.[11] I find it incredible that God not only has designed us this way but also has given us the amazing cognitive and spiritual capacities to engage in meaningful meditation.

> THROUGH MEDITATION, WE ARE ALIGNING OUR BRAINS WITH THE WORK THE HOLY SPIRIT IS DOING IN OUR HEARTS.

As a practice, biblical meditation is fairly simple, but like any other spiritual discipline it requires an investment of time and focus before it becomes a natural component of our faith-walks. There are many books and materials that address methods for biblical meditation, two of which are my book *The Soul at Rest* and Richard Foster's *A Celebration of Discipline*.[12] I will not be covering these things here; instead,

I will address some ways to help us bring our bodies, minds, hearts, and spirits together under the guidance of the Holy Spirit, so that we can succeed when we do seek to implement this practice.

## Preparing to Meditate

We can actually help our brains and make it easier to engage in the discipline of meditation if we plan ahead. We can write out what we are going to do and for how long, as well as articulate a general goal. This can be a simple statement, such as "I am going to meditate on God's Word for fifteen minutes a day during my lunch break so that I can be more peaceful and patient" or "I am going to set aside twenty minutes every morning for meditation so that I can know God more and do his will." By posting our goal where we will see it and affirming it out loud several times in advance, we will find it much easier to battle the bane of busyness in order to meet with God.

Once we've made the commitment, we need to treat our investment in meditation as a marathon, not a sprint. Most people either fail to engage consistently, or they give up too quickly on practices such as these. As we've seen, the brain is like a muscle that operates on a "use it or lose it" principle, so when we are sporadic or skip several days, it will feel as if we are starting from scratch when we return to the practice. It is better to begin with a short time commitment that we can keep, rather than a longer one we end up abandoning. Because our brains respond well to repetition, if we practice regularly, the necessary neural pathways will grow and be strengthened, and meditation will become easier to master over time.

When we actually sit down to meditate, the mental preparation to overcome distractions can seem extremely difficult. In the previous chapter I explained why this is so, and I offered practices that can counteract our wandering minds and restless souls. I personally engage in God-focused deep breathing for five to ten minutes every day before I begin my biblical meditation. (If you haven't read that chapter or tried that practice, you might want to do that first.) Here I will just note that breathing is an important component in calming our bodies and minds. When we breathe deeply, noticing how the air flows in through our nostrils and down our chests into our diaphragms, we begin to cultivate awareness, making it easier to tune out external distractions. As we concentrate on slow, deep breathing, we begin to experience a stillness within that is foundational for meditation.

Noise from without, however, is only one issue we have to deal with to prepare for meditation. As we try to calm our minds, a host of internal distractions often come up. Feelings we may not even be aware of—worry over our loved ones, fear about a job interview, frustration with our eating habits, dread from a bad dream, stresses we can't even pinpoint—suddenly surface. Curt Thompson, medical doctor and author of *The Anatomy of the Soul*, points out that while we often ignore the emotional signals—particularly unpleasant ones—that our lower brain is sending us, these are nevertheless an important part of our spiritual experience because our bodies are temples of the Holy Spirit. If we are disconnected from our feelings, we won't really be able to love God with our minds because emotions are a part of what makes up our minds. By taking a few minutes to acknowledge the feelings that come up for us, we will be more open for God to speak into our meditation.[13]

One way to do this is through journaling, an ancient spiritual practice of communing with God in writing. Journaling can be fruitful for a number of reasons. When we have a conversation with a friend, we use about 180–220 words per minute. When we type on a keyboard, we manage around 50–100 words a minute, depending on our skill level. But when we write with a pen in our journal, we have no choice but to slow down to about 30–40 words a minute. As we settle into this pace, instead of ignoring things our body may be trying to tell us (to our spiritual detriment), we can gently allow our feelings to surface, offering them to the Lord without editing or judgment, resting in the knowledge that he is intimately acquainted with all of our ways.

In the beginning, our meditation sessions may feel as if we've unleashed a tidal wave of scattered thoughts, sensations, feelings, or even intuitions. The more often we do this, however, the better able we will be to process and manage our thoughts under the gentle care of the Holy Spirit. In this way we are making space for God to reveal himself to the deepest part of us.

## Postures of the Heart in Meditation

There are three postures of the heart that many spiritual writers identify in some way as necessary for biblical meditation: humility, openness, and willingness. Thinking about these ahead of time is helpful. As we consider our coming time of meditation, we remind ourselves that being humble means recognizing that all is grace. We can't do anything to make ourselves worthy to hear God speak; he has already provided what we need. I often start my time of meditation by affirming this out loud, thanking God that I don't have to perform or get anything right, but can simply receive all that he has planned for me in these moments. Then, whether I feel far from or near to God, I thank him that he is present to meet me, and indeed that he delights to do so.

As we move into our biblical focus, we see ourselves as listeners and learners, offering to God an open heart, an inner attentiveness. Eugene Peterson reminds us of an important truth in this regard: The words of Scripture were spoken before they were written.[14] Thus, we listen for the sound of God's voice behind the words we read—the nuances and inflections, the context and emotional qualities. This is what makes meditation deeply personal. I have a small stack of letters tucked away in a chest in my bedroom, written by my father over the course of my life before he died some years ago. Every now and then I get alone and read them. When I do, I can almost hear my dad's warm, full-bodied voice, with his Southern accent and gentle concern, ringing from the words he wrote. This is a precious way for me to relive my relationship with him. In the same way, our heavenly Father speaks from every page of Scripture. If we listen carefully, we can hear the beauty of his voice and experience his presence, deepening our relationship. Hans Urs von Balthasar, a brilliant Swiss theologian and writer on prayer, describes it this way:

> I stand before my Lord, and he turns toward me personally. . . . The concrete, spoken (or silent) Word cannot be detached from the Word that he himself is. And this Word that he is does not intend merely to reach us, perhaps up to our physical or spiritual ear, but to let his words to us touch the inmost core of our person.[15]

This openness leads to the third posture of the heart: willingness. Being moved spiritually when God reveals truth to us is an important first step, but the more difficult and absolutely critical work is to consider how this revealed truth applies to our life circumstances or relationships. Simply put, once we sense that God has spoken, we engage our wills, asking things such as "Lord, what do you want me to do? How can I obey? How should this change me?" As Eugene Peterson so beautifully suggests, "We are not interested in knowing more, but in becoming more."[16]

Thus, we submit ourselves to the text of Scripture upon which we are meditating, recognizing that we do not want to remain the same. So we turn away from some vestige of human weakness or sin and take on instead the life that Jesus holds out to us.

At every step of the way in meditation, the Holy Spirit is guiding and empowering us, as our brains are being rewired in our journey toward wholeness. In this way, we are far more active participants in the transformation of our souls than we once may have thought. As Curt Thompson writes:

> OUR HEAVENLY FATHER SPEAKS FROM EVERY PAGE OF SCRIPTURE. IF WE LISTEN CAREFULLY, WE CAN HEAR THE BEAUTY OF HIS VOICE AND EXPERIENCE HIS PRESENCE, DEEPENING OUR RELATIONSHIP.

> What happens when we begin to consider that we can change the way our brains are wired? Perhaps it can point us to what God is up to when he invites us to love him and give us hope that the tools he's built inside each one of us can help us move toward lasting change.[17]

Understood in this light, biblical meditation is surely one the most important spiritual disciplines God provides for forming our souls into Christlikeness.

# BIBLICAL MEDITATION

For who knows a person's thoughts except the spirit of that person, which is in him? So also no one comprehends the thoughts of God except the Spirit of God. Now we have received not the spirit of the world, but the Spirit who is from God, that we might understand the things freely given us by God. And we impart this in words not taught by human wisdom but taught by the Spirit, interpreting spiritual truths to those who are spiritual.

1 CORINTHIANS 2:11-13

Blessed is the man
    who walks not in the counsel of the wicked,
nor stands in the way of sinners,
    nor sits in the seat of scoffers;

but his delight is in the law of the Lord,
    and on his law he meditates day and night.
He is like a tree
    planted by streams of water
that yields its fruit in its season,
    and its leaf does not wither.
In all that he does, he prospers.

PSALM 1:1-3

THERE ARE TWO PARTS TO THIS PRACTICE. The first, writing out your intention, will take fifteen to twenty minutes. How much time you spend consistently on the second part—meditation—will depend on your intention.

## Intention

Writing out our intention is a great help for our brains as we engage in a new practice. Take a few minutes ahead of time to establish your intention for meditation by prayerfully considering the following:

- *How would I like to see God work in my life as I practice biblical meditation?* Make a list, and then choose one or two things from it. What one word might capture the essence of each of these? Write it down.
- *When can I meditate? How long should I plan for?* Jot down your ideas.

Now combine these in order to write out your intention for meditation. If you prefer, you can use the following template:

Starting on [write in the day and time you intend to begin], I plan to engage in biblical meditation for [write in how much time you will spend] each session, so that I will [write in what you want to see God do within you in a few words].

Now take a few minutes to write a paragraph or two about your intention for meditation. If you want, you can write it in your journal as a prayer.

Finally, consider how you can remind yourself of this intention throughout the week. Maybe you want to put it in a reminder note on your phone or computer calendar, or post it on a sticky note on your refrigerator or bathroom mirror. The idea is to make it a visible reminder so that you can speak it aloud when you see it, helping your brain begin the preparation process.

## Heart Preparation for Meditation

On the day you are to begin your meditation, try to eliminate as many external distractions as possible. But know that you can train your mind to do this even when you are surrounded by noise. Say your intention aloud or write it at the top of the page in your journal.

*Breath.* You can begin by doing the God-focused deep breathing exercise from the last chapter, or you can engage in what is often called "spiritual breathing," in which you take in slow, deep, diaphragmatic inhalations through your nose and then exhale gently through your mouth. You may want to envision breathing in God's presence, love, kindness, hope, peace, and so on, then breathing out your restlessness, distraction, mind-wandering, and the like. Let your breaths be measured; focus on how your body feels as you slow it down.

*Feelings and thoughts.* As emotions, sensations, or thoughts come up during this time, gently let them move through your heart and mind, and offer them to the Lord for safekeeping. Don't try to analyze or edit or even judge these, but simply let God take them, knowing that he will give you what you need during this time.

*Affirmations for the heart.* Offer a prayer to the Lord based on each of the three heart postures—a prayer of humility, a prayer of openness, and a prayer of willingness. You may use the ones below or speak or write your own:

- *Humility:* Father, thank you that I can come to you as a needy child. You love and accept me, and you give me everything I need to engage in meditation on your Word.
- *Openness:* Father, I thank you that your Word is living and active. I want to listen with an open heart to what you have to say, waiting for you to show me what you have for me in this moment.
- *Willingness:* Father, my desire is to take what you show me and walk in obedience as I leave this place.

## Biblical Meditation

The following is a very simple meditation exercise. It can be used as a template for engaging with God over his Word as you begin. (See my book *The Soul at Rest* and Richard Foster's *A Celebration of Discipline* for two more thorough approaches.)

1. Choose a passage of Scripture upon which to meditate, about ten verses.
2. Read it a couple of times, including once aloud if possible.
3. Look at the passage once again and consider the words as spoken by God for you in this moment. Try to hear the words being spoken by God aloud. Consider some questions such as the following:

   • What stands out about God?

   • What do you see about yourself?

   • What is interesting or perplexing?

   • What specific words seem to come off the page?

   • What feelings does this bring up for you?

4. Ask God to speak to you concerning the words you have read. As thoughts come to you, jot them down. They may be words of encouragement, conviction, challenge, or affirmation.
5. Look back over the passage one more time and consider what difference this experience in God's Word might make in your life. Is there an action to take? An attitude to embrace? A commitment to make?

6. Write a sentence or two regarding your plan for the day or week based on what you have seen in your time of meditation. Thank God for his faithfulness.

PART THREE

# ORATIO

*The third step in lectio divina is oratio—prayer: prayer*
*understood both as dialog with God, that is, as loving conversation*
*with the One who has invited us into His embrace; and as*
*consecration, prayer as the priestly offering to God of parts of*
*ourselves that we have not previously believed God wants.*

**FR. LUKE DYSINGER,** *The Ancient Art of Lectio Divina*

# CHAPTER 06

# PRAYING THE TEXTS OF OUR DIGITAL LIVES

*When our machines overtook us, too complex and efficient for
us to control, they did it so fast and so smoothly and so usefully,
only a fool or a prophet would have dared complain.*

SIMON INGS, *Headlong*

YESTERDAY MORNING I sat in the sauna at my gym along with
seven other people. Four of them had their smartphones with
them. While a few of us chatted, those four never looked up
and never even noticed the rest of us, as far as I could tell, so
intently were they engaged with the content on the devices
in their hands. Watching them, I couldn't help but think
of a book by Christian philosopher and theologian James
K. A. Smith, in which he takes normal cultural experiences
and tries to help us see what they might suggest about our
spiritual values and priorities.

Smith asks us to imagine that some Martian anthropologists, in an attempt to gather information about our

religious habits and rituals, have visited a shopping mall. They have determined that malls are central to life in North America. Smith begins with the parking lot, suggesting that the Martians might first note the popularity of the place, given the sea of cars and number of people on "pilgrimage" (shoppers). He goes on to describe things such as the "winding labyrinth for contemplation" (the walkways between stores) or the "welcoming acolyte who offers to shepherd us through the experience" (store clerks) and the "newly minted relics" (purchases) that we leave with after we've consummated our transactions with the "priest" behind the altar (cash register).

This is not just a tongue-in-cheek metaphor, as Smith explains:

> I'm not out to be merely playful or irreverent; rather, my goal is to try to make strange what is so familiar to us precisely in order to help us see what is at stake in formative practices that are part of the mall experience. This description is meant to be apocalyptic, in a sense, unveiling the real character of what presents itself as benign.[1]

If Martian anthropologists had seen my friends in a hot sauna glued to their smartphones while surrounded by other people, what might they have assumed regarding the importance of that activity? If they were to observe your engagement with technology for a day or a week, what conclusions might they draw regarding your personal priorities or spiritual values?

Because digital interaction is ubiquitous and indispensable to our daily existence, it is difficult to step away and examine our relationship to it with a critical eye—to "make the familiar strange," as Smith would put it. But its pervasive presence is precisely why we must find a way, lest we risk shutting God out of large swaths of our lives.

*Oratio* speaks of prayer, of loving conversations with God in which we consecrate parts of ourselves that we have not previously believed he wants. In the actual practice of *lectio divina*, this step involves asking the question, *What do you want to say to me, Lord?* God surely wants to speak into our digital decisions and habits and daily rituals—things as seemingly benign as checking emails or posting on social media or texting friends or buying products online—for he alone can destroy their power to shape our identities and form our souls. This, then, is where we begin.

## What Our Practices Reveal

When I was a young girl, my mom tried in vain to teach me the proper way to make a bed, persisting for days on end. I was not a ready learner, largely because I couldn't see the point: I was only going to crawl back into bed later. Then Madeleine moved in across the street. Madeleine was young, beautiful, and newly married to a handsome businessman. She worked nights as a nurse at a local hospital. I was smitten from the start and wanted to be just like this glamorous brunette, who seemed happy to have me hang out on her days off. One morning as she was making her bed, she stopped to demonstrate the mysterious craft of folding sheets into what she called "hospital corners." As she told me how important they were for the patients she cared for, I was mesmerized by Madeleine's manicured red nails, pulling and tucking those sheet edges into pristine white curves. I wanted nothing more than to be able to do the same. We spent the better part of an hour practicing until I got it down.

I still remember my perplexed mom shaking her head when I ran into the house bragging about my newfound skill. For weeks she didn't have to tell me to make my bed because every morning I wanted to practice those lovely hospital corners—not only on my bed but on all the beds in the house.

Of course, this raises the following question: Why didn't I learn the craft of bed-making after weeks of mom's persistence, only to master it in one morning with Madeleine? Simply put, to make a bed with Madeleine was to enter into her story, one that to my young mind held the promise of beauty and romance and adventure, a story that touched some intangible longing in a little girl's heart.

This is the thing about practices: If we look at them carefully enough, we can learn something about what it is we really long for, what we believe will meet our deepest needs, what story we are choosing to live our lives by. The practices we keep, in one sense, are a window to our souls, and understanding this can help us more prayerfully consider our relationship with technology.

The story that God invites you and me into—the gospel story—transcends time and space, and it is the only one in which our deepest longings can truly be met. Yet from the time we enter this world, our culture calls us to find our joy in other narratives. From athletic excellence to academic prowess, from ageless beauty to instant popularity, from wealth to fame to power—we play our roles, energized by a way of being that Paul says is "corrupted by deceitful desires" (Ephesians 4:22, HCSB). Often oblivious, we go through our days entrenched in these sagas, embracing their habits and respecting their rituals for what we hope to gain in return.

Of course, this is nothing new. The god of this world has distorted human beings' desire for God from the start, convincing Eve that there was something more fulfilling than walking with her Maker. Yet the technological revolution has upped the ante in spades, so to speak. Not only are our waking moments now saturated with these counterfeit tales of abundant life, but the Internet also is a medium with a message and practices all its own, a medium all the more potentially destructive to our souls for its seemingly benign nature.

This is why, when we invite God to speak into our relationship with the World Wide Web, we must first wrestle with the startling degree of access that we give it to our minds and hearts. Then we need to dig deeper and uncover the stories that may be fueling our digital routines and regimens, so that we understand what is really at stake in our all-too-often mindless engagement with technology.

## Confronting the Issue of Access

We are keenly aware that digital life has its downsides. We experience the feelings of angst that come from the pressure to always be "on," to answer our cell phones no matter where we are or what we are doing, or to jump when a text comes in, as if it might carry some urgent news we can't afford to miss for one minute. We suspect, perhaps, that television's tentacles are creeping too far into our downtime and that our minds are not exactly enriched by the content we take in. We experience disturbing pangs of withdrawal when we try to set aside our digital devices. Recent research suggests that the average person checks his or her smartphone more than one hundred times per day.[2] We don't like the word *addicted*, but we know we can't live without our digital devices.

Our personal habits with our digital devices are relatively obvious to us, but they're not the whole story. Something to which we may give little thought is the potential risk in allowing external forces unfettered access to our personal lives.

While television invited corporate entities into our homes to hawk their products and promote their worldviews, the Internet ushers them into our very minds and hearts. They trawl our online activity, collecting data that they can then use not only to identify our desires but also to shape them in turn. The truth is that almost everything we do online—whether via our smartphones, tablets, cameras, computers, cars, or HDTVs—is recorded for posterity. From the restaurant we "check into" when we are having lunch to the websites we visit, from the pictures we take to the friends we choose, from what we read to what we share and whom we share it with—not just a single day but our entire history is constantly being sold to the highest bidders, who then feed the data into algorithms that create models for advertisers, which they use to target us in very specific ways. The financial stakes are high, as the entire system is set up to figure out what will grab our attention and compel us to click on an ad or a link that mysteriously appears in the top right corner of our computer screens or flashes from our smartphones or tablets when we open an app.

While these things might not seem hazardous in and of themselves—surely we can all resist an ad or link here and there—we must not underestimate the determination of the companies who buy our personal data. Their intention is to engage us, to hold our interest and keep us coming back so that we will eventually buy the commodities that keep them afloat—whether those things are something as banal as beauty things or as meaningful as political viewpoints. They don't have to get it right every time, but as computer scientist and world-renowned virtual reality scholar Jaron Lanier notes, the statistics ensure that over time their influence will intrude upon each of us. The result, Lanier laments, is a loss of freedom:

> When you carry around a smartphone with a GPS
> and camera and constantly pipe data to a computer

owned by a corporation paid by advertisers to manipulate you, you are less free. Not only are you benefiting the corporation and the advertisers, you are also accepting an assault on your free will, bit by bit.[3]

Recently, I had a conversation with a friend who used to work in the marketing department of a large telecommunications company. She shared with me about developing an advertising campaign to draw kids to their mobile television app. In their meetings, they referred to the app as a "digital pacifier." This is the kind of dependency all of us—children and adults alike—are in danger of developing through unbridled Internet usage and the access to our hearts that it provides. Click by click, frame by frame, we lose our freedom to rely on the Spirit to shape our choices, yielding instead to unseen entities with profit motives. Though we may pray or even set aside time for personal devotions, we do not live moment by moment with a Godward dependency, the kind that causes us to pause often and ask the central question of *oratio*: Lord, what do you want to say to me?

So what are we to do? We can begin by establishing a spiritual discipline of prayerful awareness whenever we are engaged with technology. When a link or an ad pops up or a friend posts some alluring video on social media, we should have a habit of pausing before we click, prayerfully asking questions such as *Is this something I need to do right now? What might the hidden agenda behind the source of this ad or link be?*

*Will clicking on this enhance or hinder my walk with God or even the work I want to accomplish?*

Beyond that, we can set goals to curtail our online hours or curb interaction with our smartphones. We can even address this using technology itself—setting reminders on our phones or computers, or downloading one of the many apps that track our usage and let us know how we're doing or that block us out of social-media sites for extended periods.

Steps like these will help, but they may not produce the kind of lasting and permanent transformation we need. For that, we must dig deeper into our online practices and patterns, exploring what they may be revealing about our hearts and the story by which we, often unconsciously, may be living our lives.

## Internet Idolatry and the Liturgies We Live

My husband and I recently saw the movie *Everest*, a tragically true spellbinder about two expeditions that encountered massive storms while attempting to scale the mountain. We left the theater asking ourselves why anyone in their right mind would devote his or her entire life to something so inherently life threatening, but a conversation between two of the men after a particularly grueling practice climb may provide some insight.

Struggling to catch his breath in the high altitude, one lamented, "This is suffering, man."

The other responded, "Few more days. [Then] for the rest of your life you'll be the guy that got to the top of Everest."

Not only were these men and women driven by a vision of mastering that mountain at the top of the world; as they pressed into the arduous training rituals and exercises, their identity became formed by that vision. They would be the ones who made it.

The reality is that we all hold certain visions of what we believe will fulfill our longings. While most aren't as grandiose as scaling Mount Everest, these visions spur us to develop habits of life—and these habits, which James K. A. Smith calls liturgies, shape and deepen our desires until the vision becomes our identity. Liturgies, in the traditional religious sense, are practices we engage in to direct our longings toward life in God's kingdom, fueled by a vision of God and his love for us. Thus, liturgies of praise or Eucharist or gratitude or confession or forgiveness or the Word are ways of practicing our part in the gospel story, forming our souls and shaping our identities: We are worshipers who find our joy in God.

Secular liturgies, on the other hand, flow from a vision rooted in some other story, one with its own set of practices and rituals. What then might be the fables behind an unrestrained engagement with digital resources? How might our online habits be directing our hearts toward desires corrupted by deceit, in the apostle Paul's words, and in turn shaping our souls or forming our identities as those who find their joy in something other than God? Here are a few possibilities:

- Incessant engagement with video games or games over social media might be a liturgy that directs our hearts and love toward achievement and competition, shaping our identities as those whose longings are met in success.
- A continual pursuit of the latest, greatest computer, smartphone, tablet, or other technological wonder might be a liturgy that directs our hearts and love toward greed, shaping our identities as those whose longings are met in material possessions.
- Posting our every move on social media or live-streaming our activity might be a liturgy that directs our hearts and love toward being noticed or admired, shaping our identities as those whose longings are met in social status.
- A voyeuristic interest in the lives of others, especially celebrities, might be a liturgy that directs our hearts and love toward a fantasy world, shaping our identities as those whose longings are met in wealth or fame.
- An obsession with technical interactions (e-mail, texts, live chats, virtual hangouts, and so on) might be liturgies that direct our hearts and love toward other people, shaping our identity as those whose longings are met in popularity, acceptance, and approval.

These are only a few, but the point here is that our Internet activity has the power to "malform" us. When our online practices direct our hearts and love toward rival gods, we are committing idolatry, a sin that not only grieves God's Spirit but also damages our souls. As Scripture shows us, when this happens, instead of becoming more like Christ, we become like the gods upon whom we have set our affections. By examining these practices, then, we may gain insight into where our desires have gone awry.

## Becoming Like Our Idols

Marshall McLuhan was a twentieth-century Canadian scholar, respected today as the original media theorist, who predicted the World Wide Web long before it came into being. McLuhan said that people who embrace the tools that technology offers, without acknowledging how they and indeed the culture at large are impacted by them, are sleepwalking through technological change. Famous for the phrase "the medium is the message," McLuhan argued that regardless of what content it might deliver, a medium itself is transformative. So, for example, because television captures our attention but doesn't require us to act in any way, it produces in us a kind of mindlessness, something brain scans have affirmed. Because the Internet sends us from link to link and willingly secures information for us, we become shallower in our thinking and plagued by attention deficit. Because social media manifests itself in sound bites with little accountability, we lose the capacity for empathy and lack sensitivity to people's real needs.

Philosopher Douglas Groothuis points out that McLuhan drew his inspiration partially from Psalm 115:4-8:

Their idols are silver and gold,
  the work of human hands.
They have mouths, but do not speak;
  eyes, but do not see.
They have ears, but do not hear;
  noses, but do not smell.
They have hands, but do not feel;
  feet, but do not walk;
  and they do not make a sound in
    their throat.
Those who make them become like them;
  so do all who trust in them.[4]

Groothuis expanded on this in an interview on how our smartphones are changing us, noting that one of the simplest yet most profound truths of Scripture is that we become like what we behold. In understanding the brain's plasticity, this makes sense. The more we gaze at something, concentrate on it, and give it our attention, the deeper the neural pathways are laid, which alters the structures of our brains. Thus, as

> AS WE FIX OUR EYES ON JESUS, AS WE GIVE HIM OUR ATTENTION AND MAKE HIM THE OBJECT OF OUR HEART'S AFFECTIONS, ... WE WILL DEVELOP NEURAL PATHWAYS THAT MATCH HIS CHARACTER.

we fix our eyes on Jesus—as we give him our attention and make him the object of our heart's affections, guided and empowered by his Spirit within us—we will develop neural pathways that match his character, and thus we will become like him.

Paul understood this many centuries ago, writing that as we behold Christ, we are "transformed into the same image from one degree of glory to another" (2 Corinthians 3:18). Groothuis unpacks this principle from a spiritual perspective:

> What we love to behold is what we worship. What we spend our time *beholding* shapes our hearts and molds us into the people we are. This spiritual truth is frightening and useful, but it raises the questions: What happens to our soul when we spend so much time beholding the glowing screens of our phones? How are we changed? How are we conformed?[5]

These are the kinds of questions that we pose through *oratio* as we bring our digital lives, our technological devices, and our virtual worlds into loving conversation with God, seeking to understand the ways in which we've somehow succumbed to idolatry, even if unaware. We must ask for spiritual revelation regarding not only the amount of time we spend beholding our digital screens but also the ways we are seeking to satisfy our souls in that space. Now, perhaps more than ever before, we must fight to secure the time and focus to allow the gentle voice of God to break through our busyness, pierce our hearts, and show us how we, driven by the technology we can't live without, are falling short of the glory for which he created us.

# EXAMEN REGARDING CORRUPTED DESIRE

And others are the ones sown among thorns. They are those who hear the word, but the cares of the world and the deceitfulness of riches and the desires for other things enter in and choke the word, and it proves unfruitful.

MARK 4:18-19

But that is not the way you learned Christ!—assuming that you have heard about him and were taught in him, as the truth is in Jesus, to put off your old self, which belongs to your former manner of life and is corrupt through deceitful desires, and to be renewed in the spirit of your minds, and to put on the new self, created after the likeness of God in true righteousness and holiness.

EPHESIANS 4:20-24

WHAT WOULD IT MEAN for you to be a good steward of the gifts of technology you have been given? How can you be certain that you are exercising dominion over them as a part of your calling according to Genesis 1:26-28? This is the purpose of the following practice.

Saint Ignatius, about whom we will learn more in chapter 8, offers a way to explore some specific weakness or sin over a period of time. We will use an adaptation of his "Particular Examen" to carefully examine our digital lives for one week, seeking to do the following three things in loving conversation with Christ and others:

1. To develop an awareness of my digital engagement, looking for any *liturgies* (patterns or practices) that demonstrate a way of being that is corrupted through deceitful desires (Ephesians 4:22).
2. To repent of seeking ultimate joy or fulfillment in any products of digital engagement (achievement, competition, popularity, escape, esteem, ownership, and so on).
3. To develop greater discipline regarding digital engagement through specific and intentional consecration of my time and habits.

Each day for one week, you will check in with God three times during the day for about five minutes each—morning, noon, and night. This particular practice will benefit greatly from interaction with others in your faith community and a level of accountability with them.

## Days One and Two

*Morning.* Spend a few minutes in prayer with God, offering him free access to your heart and your digital activity. Ask for wisdom and revelation as you go through your day. Consecrate all of your time to him to use as he wills, even hours you may be officially at work.

*Noon.* Take five minutes to look back at the morning, writing down your answers to the following questions in a journal:

- What percentage of my free time this morning was I "on" a digital device (smartphone, e-reader, tablet, TV, and so on)?
- What were the kinds of digital activities that I engaged in (surfing the Web, sending/receiving e-mails or texts, making purchases, clicking on ads or hyperlinks, and so on)?

*Before bed.* Answer the same questions you asked at noon, and jot your answers down.

- What percentage of my free time this afternoon and evening was I "on" a digital device (smartphone, e-reader, tablet, TV, and so on)?

- What were the kinds of digital activities that I engaged in (surfing the Web, sending/receiving e-mails or texts, making purchases, clicking on ads or hyperlinks, and so on)?

Review your answers to these questions and then ask God to give you wisdom regarding the following questions:

- Lord, in what ways, if any, did I seek some sort of satisfaction or fulfillment through my digital activity?
- Lord, are there any *liturgies* I engage in with my digital devices that demonstrate my love for or worship of anything other than you?

End with a time of confession and repentance as needed.

## Days Three through Seven

Continue with the same practice that you performed on days one and two, checking in with the Lord in the morning, at noon, and at night and renewing your consecration each day. In addition, begin the time before bed by considering the following question and jotting down your answer:

- Am I changing in my digital engagement as I have sought to focus on this?

You may want to continue this practice for another week, or until such time as you feel that you are no longer under technology's rule and that you are prayerfully guiding your own digital life through submission to the Spirit of God. This practice can also be a valuable periodic checkup regarding your time and involvement with technology.

CHAPTER 07

# ALONE . . . TOGETHER

*Remember, there is no such thing as an individual brain. Transformation*
*requires a collaborative interaction, with one person empathically*
*listening and responding to the other so that the speaker has the*
*experience, perhaps for the first time, of feeling felt by another.*

CURT THOMPSON, *ANATOMY OF THE SOUL*

HE MAY WELL be heralded as one of the most important people of the twenty-first century, but most of us have probably never heard of the winsome twenty-two-year-old Palmer Luckey. An upbeat homeschooler who began taking community college courses at age fourteen, Luckey loved video gaming, and he spent his free time buying and taking apart used virtual-reality headsets in his parent's garage. He wanted to see whether he could come up with something that would make his experiences more realistic. By age eighteen he'd constructed his own headset, the Oculus Rift, from scratch.

Luckey planned to sell his headset in kits for a growing crowd of gamers interested in virtual reality. Instead, his invention caught the attention of some legendary software developers. It contained technology eons beyond anything on the market. Luckey joined forces with a company to develop the Oculus Rift for the market, and eventually Facebook purchased the company (and the technology) for somewhere around two billion dollars.

What does the Oculus Rift actually do, and why is it so important? The small, goggle-like headset enables users to be completely immersed in a computer-generated environment—sort of like 3-D animation on steroids. Cory Ondrejka, Facebook's former vice president of engineering, described how this was different from anything we've ever seen: Through the use of 360-degree video cameras, we will share a sense of *place* and *presence* with others, which our brains will interpret as real, even though we are nowhere near each other. While Luckey's vision for the technology was limited to video games, Facebook's founder and CEO Mark Zuckerberg is convinced it will be the next mobile platform to saturate the world:

> Imagine enjoying a courtside seat at a game, studying in a classroom of students and teachers all over the world or consulting with a doctor face-to-face—just by putting on goggles in your home. . . . These are just some of the potential uses. By working with developers and partners across the industry, together we can build many more. One day, we believe this kind of immersive, augmented reality will become a part of daily life for billions of people.[1]

The goggles are still being fine-tuned to make them afford-able and user-friendly, but already there is a growing number of apps waiting in line that will enable the user to wander around the inside of a pyramid among the ancient ruins in Egypt or to move through virtual rooms in cyberspace along-side friends and strangers alike. Hotels have already begun providing this type of virtual service to guests; it is more than likely that this technology will soon be a regular experience for many reading this book.

How vastly our worlds will once again change as we enter this *hyper-experience* phase of the technological revolution. As exciting as it will be, now is the time for us to consider its potential impact—whether the benefits of virtual reality are going to outweigh the costs to our psyches or our relation-ships, or whether the gains of this kind of cybernetic engage-ment will turn out to be as fulfilling as the promise. Can we assume, for example, that having this incredibly tangible way of connecting, one that even our brains consider real, will deepen our interactions or create greater authenticity and closeness with each other? Will virtual reality help us build better relationships?

If we learn anything from the past, the answer is probably no. The truth is that the more choices that digital technology offers us, the more complex our lives become, further com-promising our ability to attend to each other. While we may connect in superficial ways to hundreds of people via social media, we struggle to find the time and energy for meaning-ful personal interactions with even a handful of close friends.

Regularly feeling depleted, we too often opt for the convenient lure of digital contact (texting supersedes talking), rather than investing in real-time, face-to-face engagement with others. The cumulative losses of this are egregious to our souls and particularly so in our pursuit of authentic Christianity. From God's perspective, spiritual formation can never be relegated to a solo endeavor. *Oratio*—loving conversations with God that lead to greater consecration—is deeply meaningful in times alone with God, but practicing it together is an indispensable component of any Christ follower's formation in his image.

## Formed in Community

Perhaps no group, with the exception of the nuclear family, suffers more keenly from the consequences of digital overuse than communities of faith, in which relationships are the very currency of spiritual growth. The problem is obscured, however, by a false sense of living out our spiritual destiny through cyber-connections. Believers can partake of a church service by themselves almost any day of the week via their computers, smartphones, or TV screens; keep up with the very latest in worship music online from their living rooms; receive powerfully written devotional blogs daily at their desks via

> FROM GOD'S PERSPECTIVE, SPIRITUAL FORMATION CAN NEVER BE RELEGATED TO A SOLO ENDEAVOR.

e-mail; participate in inspirational causes by "liking" pages on social media; and join others in Bible studies and prayer groups through specialized apps. While these things and dozens more like them may be valuable tools for aiding our spiritual growth, they only seem relational; in actuality they take place in isolation. They can never replace the kinds of embodied relationships for which we are made.

When our Trinitarian God—Father, Son, and Holy Spirit—launched the human story with "Let us make man in our image" (Genesis 1:26), he established the pattern of communal life, and so it has always been. Our spirituality flourishes amongst the pulsating presence of others. This means that the Christian journey is uniquely incarnational: Not only did the Word become flesh and dwell among us, but together we also become the tangible, physical presence—the *embodiment*—of Christ on this earth. We must never take this lightly or let its beautiful mystery get buried in the busyness of our hyperconnected lives, for as Douglas Groothuis reminds us, "When the flesh becomes data it fails to dwell among us."[2]

As members of a collective—the body of Christ in this world—we thrive through the physicality of being together. Paul yearned for this, writing to the Thessalonians that he felt as if he'd been torn from them and that his desire to see them face-to-face consumed him with earnest prayer day and night (1 Thessalonians 2:17; 3:10). The aging apostle John wrote that although for a time he was limited to writing letters, he hoped soon to be face-to-face with his family of faith "so that our joy may be complete" (2 John 1:12). Truth be told, we all long for and need this kind of communion, whether we realize it or not. Not only does interacting face-to-face with others enhance the well-being of our souls, but as it turns out, our brains are also actually wired for it.

## There Is No Single Brain

My son and his family care for foster babies. I remember well when they brought baby Gina into their home. The back of her head was completely flat, an indication that she'd been left alone lying face up for the bulk of her young life. Placid to the extreme, baby Gina rarely cried; instead, she spent hours staring blankly at the ceiling. This didn't last long, however. Once my son, his wife, two sets of grandparents, four siblings, and a host of friends began to love on her, the metamorphosis was amazing to behold. Gina quickly became a laughing, cooing, kicking, wide-eyed image of content-ment, entertaining us all with her antics for months to come.

Attachment theory tells us that Gina, like all babies, came into the world looking for connections—her brain could not develop properly without it. Her initial lack of interactivity reflected what she had failed to receive in her early months. This is why it is said that there is no such thing as an indi-vidual brain. Our neural networks have been established through hundreds of experiences that began when we were infants in relationship with our mothers or fathers or other caregivers. Given the plasticity of our brains, our interactions with others will continue to shape how we see ourselves, other people, and the world in which we live for the rest of our lives.[3]

Simply put, each of us is "a story wrapped in skin."[4] Our stories are inscribed on the neural pathways located largely in our prefrontal cortex. All of our lives we look to others, not only to make sense of what we experience but also to help us rewrite the pages in us that are flawed because of painful life circumstances or relationships. Even what we think we know of God has been formed through life in a fallen world. As a result, we need authentic and vulnerable connections with other believers in order to really know God. As Christian psychiatrist Curt Thompson explains, "Your relationship with God is a direct reflection of the depth of your relationship with others."[5]

For years I believed that God needed me to "get the job done" and that his acceptance and approval rose and fell based on how well I was doing it. As an adult, I began to see that a biblical understanding of grace didn't support this view of me or God, so I tried hard to change. But I couldn't dislodge that deep-seated propensity to perform with God or others. One night I voiced my frustration to my husband, telling him that I didn't know what to do if God didn't need me. He smiled and said, "That's just it: You really can't do anything, can you?"

This wasn't the answer I wanted, and the next morning I sat before God in tears, terrified at my growing feelings of vulnerability. After a time, I ventured out to try and share with my husband, but I couldn't even articulate how I felt as we sat on the couch together. So he simply held me as I cried, and then at some point he looked me in the eyes and said tenderly, "Tricia, God doesn't need you, but he wants you."

I was undone. Later that morning, a friend came over and, in essence, spoke the same truth to my soul. This was the beginning of my new story, my new ability to experience God's affection for me as his precious child, who didn't have to perform to enjoy his love.

Heart-to-heart connections like these—connections that can alter our faulty stories, rewire our neural circuitry, and form us as Christ followers—won't happen through snippets in texts or likes on social-media pages or even by entering into each other's virtual reality. Person-to-person, face-to-face, embodied communion is essential for the kinds of bonds that God has afforded uniquely to human beings.

## Mirror Neurons and Digital Relating

One of the more fascinating discoveries in brain science is the existence of what are called mirror neurons. These neurons fire when we observe someone else doing a specific action, as if we were doing it ourselves. For example, when you see a mother pushing a stroller, neurons fire in your brain almost as if you were actually pushing the stroller yourself. When we notice that someone is hurt—physically or emotionally—the mirror neurons in our brains simulate their experience for us as well, enabling us to empathize with them. Mirror neurons also trigger humor in us when we hear another person laugh, which is why laughter can be so contagious. The emotional component to mirror neurons is an amazing gift that has been given only to human beings. Only we can feel each other's sadness or pain or happiness.

But we are called to move beyond feeling to acting—to rejoice with those who rejoice and weep with those who weep (Romans 12:15), to be tenderhearted toward each other (Ephesians 4:32), and to bear one another's burdens (Galatians 6:2). For this to happen, we need to be *present* to each other, something extremely difficult via digital engagement. Why? Between 60 and 90 percent of the time we communicate our feelings in nonverbal ways—through the expressions on our face, eye contact, physical touch, the inflections in our voice, or our body language. Whether we are the ones experiencing the emotion or the ones empathizing with it, we are dependent to a great degree on nonverbal cues, which easily get lost in a digital environment. Emojis and emoticons are sorely insufficient substitutes for heartfelt expressions.

I experienced this in a profound way years ago when e-mail was in its nascent stages. A friend wrote to me of how he was feeling directionless and without hope. While I felt sad for him and wanted to help carry his burden, I had no idea of the depth of his struggle. I assumed he wanted advice, so I gave it.

My concern and support did not come across in my e-mail. In my prosaic and rapid response, he heard only judgment. He responded by saying, "I was looking for a friend, not a judge and jury."

In that moment I realized that there were some things that could never be meaningfully shared without person-to-person contact, and I determined never again to use e-mail to communicate anything of a sensitive nature. While digital engagement can surely augment our interpersonal connections, it is inadequate at best. At worst, its sterile structure can be dangerous to the well-being of our souls and of those we love. The more we are immersed in our cyber-worlds, the easier it is to lose sight of this; in the process, we end up squandering something of our own humanness.

> WHILE DIGITAL ENGAGEMENT CAN SURELY AUGMENT OUR INTERPERSONAL CONNECTIONS, IT IS INADEQUATE AT BEST.

## Losing Our Humanness

In her sobering book *Alone Together*, sociologist Sherry Turkle writes of how digital devices have led to a new kind of self, one that has been "wired into existence through technology."[6] It is a self, she contends, that is split between the virtual and the real, and as a result the lines between them are continually blurred. She shares the example of teenagers for whom the cell phone is almost a "phantom limb": They sleep with their phones and sense them vibrating, even if the phones are shut up in their lockers at school. Digital natives who have grown up with technology at their fingertips from birth don't necessarily view the virtual world as separate or even secondary to their existence but literally as a part of who they are.

As a digital immigrant, I do know, at least from life experience, how very distinct these two ways of being—online and offline—really are. And yet I, too, struggle with the boundaries. I find myself posting pictures on social media although I've been too busy to visit with a neighbor. I have gotten into the habit of placing my cell phone on the table when having a meal with a friend, as if digital interruptions supersede real-time conversations. Recently, a family in our church lost a child, and while I hope that the mom's posting of pictures and painful struggles on social media is therapeutic and helpful, I have to wonder how many of us assume that we've shown true compassion by pressing the "like" button or commenting with some inspirational quote or verse. What is *real* and what is *virtual* in this hyperlinked life of ours?

On the one hand, we can never underestimate the benefits technology has wrought, even to relationships. I connect more now with some old friends and family members than I ever did before, simply because the Internet makes it so easy. I interact often with fellow believers from across the globe and have been blessed to make acquaintances with people I would never have met otherwise. Yet when relationships are reflected by friend counts on social media, when face-to-face conversations are supplanted by tweets and texts that we edit and delete, when we would rather swipe an app than sit quietly with a hurting friend, when we prefer superficial snippets of information over the messy complexities of relating in real time, what of our humanness are we in danger of losing? What of God's image in us is slowly being extinguished as we rely more and more on technology and less on the gentle whisper of his voice, of his Spirit wooing our spirits to reach out and really touch each other?

In an assessment based on research into our digital lives by the Barna Group, Jun Young and David Kinnaman suggest that the most disturbing thing about this slow slip into the dominance of hyperlinked relationships is that at some point we won't really want anything different—it will be too much of a bother.[7] Indeed, we all face a growing penchant to bond with technology—becoming inseparable from our smartphones, valuing our computers more than our business associates, or feeling like we have some sort of personal relationship with reality-show characters we've never met. As Sherry Turkle points out, at some point people will simply stop caring about the loss of real relationship, having "come to see our online life as life itself. . . . It becomes what we want. These seem the gathering clouds of a perfect storm."[8]

It seems to me that those gathering clouds are growing darker by the day as technology produces further opportunities for us to blur the lines between the virtual and the real in relationships. This brings me back to the start of this chapter. Is it possible that the clouds will burst when the Oculus Rift comes crashing into our homes—when billions of us, if Facebook has its way, begin to use it to engage with our world every single day? Will we be tempted to replace embodied fellowship with cyber-groups or congregational worship with techno-events, neither of which demands anything from us since we never have to leave the security of our isolated worlds?

If so, then how should we as Christ followers prepare? How can we prepare to fight against losing the very qualities that make us human, that enable us to be Christ's eyes and ears and hands and feet—for each other and the world—in ways that machines simply never can be? These are conversations we need to be having together in God's presence, seeking his wisdom.

## Monasticism and Table Talk

Many of us do feel the discomfort of digital dominance in our lives. In a recent survey conducted by Desiring God, almost 40 percent of the eight thousand respondents ages eighteen to thirty-nine agreed with the following statement: "My use of social media is uncontrolled and unhealthy. I check my social networks compulsively throughout the day, and it's probably not good for me."[9] This is the generation that has grown up with the Net, the ones who hold the future in their hands. While only 21 percent of older generations agreed with the statement above, it is going to take all of us making hard choices if we really want to turn the tide of technological tyranny. I believe that as the family of God, our life together depends on it.

In his book *Desiring the Kingdom*, James K. A. Smith

suggests a unique approach to counteracting the constant pressure of cultural liturgies—many of which, as I pointed out in the last chapter, relate to our networked existence. Specifically, he calls for a sort of monasticism, though not by withdrawing, as we might normally think. Instead, he suggests that we reimagine for today's world two characteristics of monastic life that could be formative for us.

The first has to do with abstaining from certain cultural practices that others would consider normal, not in order to pull away from the culture itself but to reject specific structures that may be detrimental to our spiritual health.[10] For example, we might decide to abstain from social media, at least for periods of time, because as a cultural liturgy, it fosters self-absorption and shallow relationships. In its place, we would seek to find more meaningful and embodied ways to engage with people. Or we might decide to abstain from all screen activity for segments of time each week—perhaps evenings or weekends—because as a cultural liturgy, being glued to our computers, TVs, or smartphone screens fosters insensitivity, mindlessness, and weak faith. In its place, we would seek to focus more on the world around us—going for walks with friends, having face-to-face conversations with family members, or praying or studying with others. In a similar suggestion, spiritual formation professor Bruce Hindmarsh calls for some in the body of Christ to become "digital monks," to take lengthy sabbaticals from media in every way possible, and then share with the rest of us what they learn from the process.[11]

How might these or other examples of abstention from cultural liturgies address our need for *oratio*—loving conversations together in God's presence that lead to greater consecration? Most importantly, they open up space for us to consider what has been at stake and what we are in danger of losing. Stepping away from digital life, even for a time, removes the barriers of distraction that often lead to fragmented connections with the people in our lives. Freed from the tedium of incessant interruptions, we can experience afresh the power and beauty in embodied relationships, something we may not have even realized we were missing. As we develop the discipline of *presence*, we begin to honor and attend to the people around us, opening ourselves up to the wonder of *koinonia*, the building of spiritual community.[12]

This leads to the second idea that Smith draws from monasticism, which is establishing rhythms of daily worship that "are holistic, activating the imagination through bodily participation."[13] These do not have to take place in structured church services, although Smith describes some communities who are seeking to do just that. Instead, he points out that formative habits and spiritual disciplines can take place in far less formal settings—at our kitchen tables, for example. Hindmarsh agrees, noting that "it is no accident that Christ left us with a meal. Meeting face-to-face around a meal is a radical context for discipleship."[14]

This suggestion is heartily affirmed by theologian and church historian Leonard Sweet, who wrote an entire book on the topic. In *From Tablet to Table*, he makes the sweeping claim that just by sharing our stories in the context of a meal together, we will strengthen our families, breed faith in our children, and form our identity as the people of God. Indeed, he declares that "the most important thing anyone can do to change our world for the better is to bring back the table— with Jesus seated at his rightful place."[15]

The table takes center stage at some point in each episode of one of my favorite TV shows. Spanning three generations of law enforcement, the family at the center of *Blue Bloods* includes a retired New York chief of police, the current chief, his daughter (a district attorney), his two sons—one of whom is a married detective and the other a single beat cop—and three children. Each week the storylines follow two or three of the characters in their respective jobs. These storylines are often unrelated, but the show always culminates in a family meal. Dad leads out in a prayer of grace from the head of the table, and the meal commences, with food and drink passed back and forth amidst noisy chatter about each member's life experiences. Young and old alike pass on their stories, share lessons, challenge ideas, and offer advice as this family participates in what clearly has been a tradition for generations.

Although the segment only represents a tiny portion of each episode, I always find myself waiting for the family meal. I know somehow that everything else will make sense once the family brings it together around the dining room table, for the storyline that undergirds all the rest is that of a family who depend on each other and find their joy in being together.

This is such a beautiful picture of how we, the body of Christ, can practice *oratio*. On a practical level, it demonstrates that as we invest the time and energy in embodied relationships through things like having a meal together, we make sense of our own stories, finding in our brothers and sisters what we really need to pursue God's kingdom. But it is more than that. As a metaphor, it reminds us how our heavenly Father delights in gathering his children so that we can commune together. There, with Jesus at the head of the table, we share in the joy of being his family and living the real life he has planned for us. As Sweet suggests, "At the table, Jesus moves us from ideas about life and love to actual living and loving."[16]

This is what we have to gain by helping each other regularly recalibrate our digital lives. Breaking bread together as families or small groups or congregations—in homes, restaurants, coffee shops, or neighborhood parks—creates the kinds of environments where *oratio* feels good and right, environments that even the most advanced virtual reality can never reproduce. Loving conversations in the presence of God around a meal, leading to greater consecration—this is the most ancient of spiritual practices, ever holding out the promise of deeper real-life relationships.

# A BRIEF AND PRAYERFUL ASSESSMENT

For I long to see you so that I may impart some
spiritual gift to you, that you may be established;
that is, that I may be encouraged together with you
while among you, each of us by the other's faith,
both yours and mine.

ROMANS 1:11-12, NASB

THE PURPOSE OF THIS BRIEF PRAYER PRACTICE is to examine your relationships as they exist within your virtual and nonvirtual worlds and to establish an action plan for improvement.

### Step One

Settle your heart before the Lord, engaging in God-focused deep breathing (see chapter 4) or in other methods you've experienced that bring your mind and spirit together with an awareness of God's presence.

### Step Two

Ask the Holy Spirit to guide this time, to open your mind and heart, and to be tangibly present throughout your assessment. Submit yourself to the Lord.

### Step Three

The following items are a series of explorations for you to bring before the Lord. Jot down your answers in a journal, but be brief—usually the first thing that comes to your mind is all you need to write.

- What are the names of the people with whom I share my personal journey on a regular basis (one to three of your closest relationships)?
- How many times per week am I in contact with them

via technology (texting, calls, social media, e-mails, and so on)?

- How many times per week am I in contact with them personally (face-to-face conversations)?
- What areas of my life do I share openly and vulnerably with these people?
- What areas of my life do I tend to withhold from sharing with these people?

## Step Four

Look back over your answers and then pray through the following questions, asking the Spirit to speak to your heart and jotting notes in your journal.

- How has technology enhanced my closest relationships?
- Do I rely on technology for connections rather than taking the time and making the effort to reach out to my close friends and family? If so, how often?
- What might it mean to go deeper in these relationships —to be more present personally and to share more vulnerably in order to give and receive encouragement in our journeys?

## Step Five

Based on your answers above, write out a prayer of commitment to God and to yourself regarding how you want to pursue deeper connections with others, and what that will look like. Be as specific as possible with the steps you plan to take.

## Step Six

Prayerfully choose at least one person with whom you will share this practice and your experience, asking them to walk alongside you as you seek to implement the things God has revealed.

# TABLE-TALK CONNECTIONS

ESTIMATED TIME: 2-3 HOURS

Therefore encourage one another and build each other up, just as you are doing.

1 THESSALONIANS 5:11

From him the whole body, joined and held together by every supporting ligament, grows and builds itself up in love, as each part does its work.

EPHESIANS 4:16, NIV

THE PURPOSE OF THIS PRACTICE is to join with a small group of people who are fairly close to you in order to discuss some of the things you've learned in this chapter, as well as to encourage each other through affirmations that help rewire faulty neural pathways.

## Preparation

Set a time and date for a simple meal (a potluck works great). Invite a handful of family and friends (a maximum of six people) with whom you feel you can be yourself—this could be a small group you are already a part of. Feel free to include kids or even to do this with your family, but consider adjusting the format some if you do. Ask older teenagers and adults to read this chapter sometime before your gathering and to jot down two or three things they found interesting about relating together. Have enough note cards on hand for group members to share with each other (so, for example, if your group has six members, you will need thirty-six cards).

## During the Meal

While you eat, talk about the things in this chapter that stood out to each of you. Maintain a relaxed, conversational environment, but when necessary, rein the discussion in and direct it back toward the topic of connecting with each other.

## After the Meal

While still at the table (perhaps over dessert and coffee), remind everyone briefly about how our brains form faulty neural pathways based on life experiences, and how we can help each other rewire these pathways with the guidance of God's Spirit. First, ask members to think of something about themselves that they tend to dislike or struggle to accept. After they've had a few minutes to think, do the following:

1. Have one person share his or her answer.
2. Give the group two minutes of prayerful silence while each member thinks of an affirmation to offer this person regarding his or her answer. During this time, you will quietly listen to your hearts and the Spirit in order to have something to share. You will write your affirmations down on note cards to give to the person. People may write down words of encouragement, Scripture, expressions of affection, or something else. The person who is being prayed for may also receive something during this silence, so encourage him or her to write this down as well.
3. After two minutes have passed, go around the table and have each person speak his or her affirmation to this person.
4. Ask the person to give a brief response regarding what these things mean to him or her.
5. Repeat the process with each group member.

6. End with a brief prayer confirming the work of God's Spirit in your hearts.

Encourage members to read their cards every day for the next month as they work on this area in their lives.

PART FOUR

# CONTEMPLATIO

*The life of contemplation is perforce an everyday life, of
small fidelities and services performed in the spirit of love,
which lightens our tasks and gives to them its warmth.*

**HANS URS VON BALTHASAR,** *Prayer*

# CHAPTER 08

# THE CONTEMPLATIVE LIFE

*The contemplative tradition suggests that to be so acutely
aware of God's beauty in anything leads to awareness of
God's beauty in everything, save that which is evil.*

**CURT THOMPSON,** *Anatomy of the Soul*

ON THE DAY Iñigo Lopez was born to a wealthy Basque family in 1491, the Spanish Inquisition was rounding up Jews, Muslims, and others to burn at the stake. A young German boy named Martin Luther was playing with his brothers and sisters in the quaint mountain town of Mansfeld. And an audacious Italian explorer named Christopher was making final preparations for his imminent journey to the New World. Oblivious to the monumental seeds of change being sewn all around them, Iñigo's aristocratic parents pampered their beloved son until he turned fifteen and took his first job as a page in the royal court. Soon bored with that, the handsome young man entered the military, where he quickly became known for his roguish lifestyle and valiant exploits. Had it not been for a battle with the French for a town named Pamplona, in which he was hit in both legs by cannonballs, Iñigo Lopez would perhaps have never made the annals of history—and we, as Christ followers, might have missed out on some of the richest and most practical resources ever written for the faith journey. Hospitalized for seven weeks while undergoing numerous surgeries, Iñigo pored over the only books available—books by and about saints of old. Soon he had a series of spiritual experiences that would lead him to devote his life to Christ and eventually to write. His *Spiritual Exercises*, a four-week journey of prayer, meditation, and contemplation, continues to be relevant and life-changing for Christians across denominations today.[1]

Iñigo, known today as Ignatius of Loyola, founded a monastic order he called "the company of Jesus," teaching them how to be "contemplatives in action" by knowing and loving God so intimately that they would see him in all things as they lived and worked in the world. Today this order, known as the Jesuits, has some twenty thousand members in 112 nations. They are known and respected for their scholarship, as well as for their commitment to obeying Ignatius's mandate. The official Jesuit website describes Ignatian spirituality as "not merely an inward journey, much less a self-absorbed one. It aims to bring people closer to God and more deeply into the world—with gratitude, passion, and humility—not away from it."[2]

There is perhaps no way of being in this world more at

risk today than the contemplative one. While the drumbeat of the digital age beats with immediacy and speed, contemplative living is rooted in the slow momentum of time. While technology is, by nature, designed to increase efficiency, contemplatives often pursue a path that can appear patently unproductive. While expediency fuels the cyber-life, contemplatives are energized by the sacredness in ordinary moments. And while our Web-saturated existences can reduce relationships to instant messages and images on social media, living contemplatively calls for ever-deepening connections both with God and with others. Although this divide does not necessarily keep contemplatives from full immersion in today's techno-world, it requires a high level of focused intentionality to do so.

More on that later. But first, what exactly is a contemplative? The term is used today in the public sphere in everything from TED Talks to blogs to mainstream news to academic journal articles. Indeed, there are now contemplative neuroscience departments at several major universities. Perhaps because the conversation is less common in Christian (particularly Protestant) circles, there is no widespread agreement on what a contemplative life might look like. On the one hand, spiritual leaders like Richard Foster warn spiritual novices away from contemplation, noting that it is a form of prayer "for those who have exercised their spiritual muscles a bit and know something about the landscape of the Spirit."[3] On the other hand, Eugene Peterson suggests that there is nothing really special about contemplation: It is "the Christian life, nothing more but also nothing less. But *lived.*"[4] This, then, is where we begin.

## Understanding Contemplative Life

How do you define the indefinable? How do you describe the ineffable? How do you pinpoint the parts of a process that defies delineation? How do you put into words an experience that can seem as rare and exquisite as the finest of wines, yet as important to faith as air to our lungs? These questions plagued me as I prepared to write this chapter. Even my spiritual mentors, those wise saints who have written throughout the centuries and whose books have guided me on my journey, tend to talk about contemplation in diverse ways—and at times, as I've noted, they are at odds regarding its purpose.

I confess, then, that I feel quite inadequate for this task. I have an evolving grasp of contemplation based on my own journey and years of reading, but I am keenly aware that the things I write will likely frustrate some who prefer a more didactic approach while causing contemplative purists to shake their heads at my naiveté. To that end, reader beware—what more can I say?

For many people, the word *contemplation* conjures up images of silent saints in serene settings, transfixed by the presence of God. Indeed, one of Webster's definitions of the term is "a state of mystical awareness of God's being." Unfortunately, this limited view has been singularly promoted by many scholars and spiritual guides in centuries past and present, and while it is accurate as far as it goes, it fails to capture the breadth of contemplation as a lifestyle for people of faith.[5] Contemplation does indeed make us more aware of the reality of God's loving presence for ourselves. But it also causes us to see our world and the people in it in ways we never could otherwise.

This gift of sight—of understanding that comes only by divine revelation—is a central theme in much writing and teaching about contemplation. In fact, one of the early desert fathers, Evagrius, called contemplation a *theoria physike*, which literally means "a vision into the nature of things." Based on this under-

> CONTEMPLATION DOES INDEED MAKE US MORE AWARE OF THE REALITY OF GOD'S LOVING PRESENCE FOR OURSELVES. BUT IT ALSO CAUSES US TO SEE OUR WORLD AND THE PEOPLE IN IT IN WAYS WE NEVER COULD OTHERWISE.

standing, Henri Nouwen concludes that "the contemplative life, therefore, is not a life that offers a few good moments between the many bad ones, but a life that transforms all of our time into a window through which the invisible world becomes visible."[6]

Another common theme related to the contemplative life is that it springs from a supernatural experience of God's love. Thus, John of the Cross calls contemplation "a secret and peaceful and loving inflow of God."[7] Another teacher explains, "Christic contemplation is nothing less than a deep love communion with the triune God. By *depth* here we mean a knowing love that we cannot produce but only receive."[8] At the risk of oversimplification, I would like to suggest that Christian contemplatives are those for whom a vision of God's love both infuses and informs the whole of their lives. To explore this further, let me try to untangle what I believe are some of the myths about contemplation.

## Myths about Contemplation

First, I do not believe that contemplation is reserved for people who have reached a certain level of maturity in their faith. While the intimate knowledge of God evolves over the course of one's lifetime, anyone who has entered into a relationship with Christ can be captivated by a vision of his unfathomable love, not merely in theory or by faith but through personal experience. My first taste came when I was nineteen years old, as I stood outside a gas station with an older aunt who challenged me to fall in love with Jesus. Her words arrested my heart, and I felt as if a gentle breeze were wafting over my entire being. Now, decades later, I can see that in that moment I drank the tiniest drop from an infinite river, but it was more than enough for me to know that my life would never be the same.

Second, contemplation is *nurtured by* but not *relegated to* times of solitude and silence. As I will show later, in order to live contemplatively we do need times of withdrawal when we are alone with nothing more than our own hearts and the God of the universe. But this does not mean that we leave all of this behind when we venture out of our solitude. Indeed, to be contemplative means to live and move and have our being in the ebb and flow of God's love, allowing it to soften our hearts and open our eyes—whether we are far from the madding crowd or embroiled in the noisy chaos of our daily existence.

Third, the fruit of contemplation is not something that we achieve by our own merit, spiritual prowess, or even discipline. While some practices can help us prepare our hearts and we can do certain things to make ourselves more spiritually aware, only God can open the eyes of our hearts and shed his love within them (Romans 5:5). He alone determines how and when he will do so. As he reveals himself across the seasons of our spiritual journey—when we stumble and when we stand, in the dry times and the dark times, through the joyous celebrations and the agonizing losses—we will know more and more of this love that is beyond understanding (Ephesians 3:19-21).

The truth is, however, that while living contemplatively spurs us to cultivate obedience, this does not make us worthy of a vision of God's love; nor—on the other hand—do our weaknesses keep us from receiving it, for as Eugene Peterson reminds us, "all contemplatives are failed contemplatives."[9]

Finally, although there may be times when we're so taken with the beauty of God that we feel as if we've been transported to some other realm (for example, Paul's vision of the third heaven in 2 Corinthians 12:1-6), far more often contemplation entails glimpses of God's love in momentary interludes. This can happen as we drive to work or kneel in glorious worship. It can surprise us as we are offering a sandwich to a homeless person or gathering to pray with friends or kissing our kids good night or savoring a moment in God's Word. We can't hold on to it when it happens, and we may struggle to put our experience into words. But in some way, as we taste and see that God is good, we know in our heart of hearts not only that are we loved but also that his love bathes our world and the people in it. These joys, though almost imperceptible, become the defining moments of our days.

## Living Contemplatively

Contemplative living is best understood as a cycle that flows from action to inaction, movement to stillness, crowds to solitude, and back again. Pulling away to spend time alone is the pause, the rest note, the Sabbath of time, energy, and activity that enables us to fix our hearts on the living God. These moments, however, are never meant to foster ingrown introspection. Rather, God's engagement across our busy lives runs like a gentle undercurrent through our times of silence, like the translucent stillness of a pond kept from stagnation by underground streams. Our experience of his loving embrace in that place carries us from our solitude back into "the midst of an anxious and violent world as a sign of hope and a source of courage."[10] We don't come by any of this naturally; we need patience, persistence, and a large measure of grace to flourish in the contemplative current.

## Contemplation in Solitude

Solitude and silence are rare commodities in an age of perpetual motion, constant connection, and the unyielding pressure to multitask the moments of our days. Not only have we become habituated to compulsive activity, but, as I've noted throughout the book, the neural pathways in our brains that support things like quietness and contemplation are growing weaker as more and more of our lives become digitized. As a result, we are losing our capacity for *rest, reflection*, and *resonance*, all of which are central to the kind of meaningful existence for which God created and redeemed us.

The good news is that, although it will take time and commitment, we really can rewire our brains to recapture these indispensable gifts by pressing into the practice of private contemplation in God's presence.

*Rest.* To rest—our first need in contemplation—means to put aside the noisy chaos without and within in order to connect authentically with God. Augustine, in his teaching on the Ten Commandments, calls this a "Sabbath in the heart," and notes how hard it can be:

> God is saying, "Be still and see that I am God." But you, so restless, refuse to be still. You are like the Egyptians tormented by gnats. These, the tiniest of flies, always restless, flying about aimlessly, swarm at your eyes, giving no rest. They are back as soon as you drive them off. Just like the futile fantasies

that swarm in our minds. Keep the commandment,
beware of the plague.[11]

We all can probably relate to this and to the words of Rowan
Williams, former Archbishop of Canterbury, who com-
mented that "the deepest problem in prayer is often not
the absence of God but the absence of me. I'm not actually
there. My mind is everywhere."[12] Resting requires that we
rein in all of our thoughts and emotions so that we can be
present to God in the moment. This Sabbath in the heart
is where we want to remain, lingering in the stillness as we
silently commune with the One who delights to spend time
with us.

Rest also means learning to let go of our need to impress
or our effort to achieve, so that we can just be ourselves. For
those of us who are used to playing out our lives in public
on the digital stage, this is extremely difficult, and yet the
struggle is not a new one. The writer of Hebrews explains
that "whoever has entered God's rest has also rested from his
works," but then he offers the paradoxical refrain: "Let us
therefore strive to enter that rest" (Hebrews 4:10-11). This is
the conundrum of rest—we are to move from *doing* to *being*,
from *trying* to *relying*, from *activity* to *passivity*, but we have
to exert all of our energy to do so.

Contemplation calls for us to let go of our need to accomplish something in times alone with God. We must strive for
this because it feels so foreign to our normal way of thinking, especially about prayer. The moment we seek to do

nothing but enjoy God's presence, our egos fuss and fidget, and we feel the pressure to produce. Years ago I shared about contemplation with a group of missionaries, and one reacted incredulously, insisting that she could never waste time that way when she had so many people and needs on her daily prayer list. But resting means just that: wasting time on God himself— not on what he might do for us

> THE MOMENT WE SEEK TO DO NOTHING BUT ENJOY GOD'S PRESENCE, OUR EGOS FUSS AND FIDGET, AND WE FEEL THE PRESSURE TO PRODUCE.

or in us or through us, but on him alone. Marva Dawn calls this "a total waste of time in earthly terms, a total immersion in the eternity of God's infinite splendor for the sole purpose of honoring God."[13]

*Reflection.* From the place of rest we move to the second component of contemplation in solitude: reflection. Unlike in meditation, where we seek to focus our minds on eternal truths, here we simply seek to love God himself. Henri Nouwen calls solitude the "place of the great encounter," noting that here God reveals himself "as the God who wants to give himself to us with an unconditional, unlimited and unrestrained love, and as the God who wants to be loved by us with all our heart, all our soul and all our mind."[14] As we connect with God's tender countenance, as we taste and see that he is good and that his loving-kindness is truly better than life, we cannot help but want to love him back— silently, wordlessly, effortlessly. This kind of encounter is what makes contemplation transforming, but it takes time; you really cannot rush love.

A transforming vision of God's love is rooted in our realization that he is not only transcendent but immanent. Thus, the miracle of the indwelling Christ is the very core of contemplation. Augustine helps us here again: "Why do we rush about to the top of heaven and the bottom of earth, looking for him who is here at home with us, if only we could be at home with him?" And then, "Return to your heart! See there what you perceive about God because the image of God is there."[15] As we pull away from life's mesmerizing minutiae and begin to envision Christ as our ever-present companion, his whispers of love become beams of light, warming the caverns of our hearts from the inside out. This is the fruit of reflection.

In 1912, a pharmacist turned publisher named C. Austin Miles opened his Bible to John 20 and was captivated by the story of Mary at Jesus' tomb. Soon the wall of his room faded away, and he saw a garden in his mind's eye where a woman in white wept, clasping her throat to hold back sobs. He goes on to unfold the story of Peter and John coming and going, and then the moment when Mary saw Jesus. Lost in this encounter, Miles felt he was personally seeing Christ in all his glory as well. He described what happened next:

> I awakened in sunlight, gripping the Bible, with
> muscles tense and nerves vibrating. Under the
> inspiration of this vision I wrote as quickly as the
> words could be formed the poem exactly as it has

since appeared. That same evening I wrote the music.[16]

The poem Miles refers to here became the well-known hymn "In the Garden." While it unveils a beautiful picture of the kind of encounter one has with Christ in contemplation—"He walks with me and talks with me and tells me I am his own"— Miles ends with this:

> *I'd stay in the garden with Him*
> *Though the night around me be falling,*
> *But He bids me go; through the voice of woe,*
> *His voice to me is calling.*

As wonderful as times of contemplation are in God's presence, his voice will always call us to go. As this happens, we experience the third phase of our journey in solitude, that of *resonance.*

*Resonance.* Resonance is what happens when our hearts, vibrating with God's love, understand anew why we are on this earth. As our eyes are lifted to our ordinary world and the day before us, rather than feeling fear or anxiety or a need to control, we experience a deep and personal sense of meaning about even the smallest details. Sven Birkerts suggests that resonance is what we miss when cyber-time is our perpetual reality—this propensity to ponder how the things we do and the way we live actually matters in the grand scheme of things, this awareness that there is an order and a sense of coherence to the world that transcends us.[17] Resonance is a sorely needed quality for us as Christ followers today: It prepares us to move about the world into which Jesus sends us. In other words, resonance spurs us to be contemplatives in action.

### Contemplation as We Go

Yesterday as I was warming up in my gym's spa, I was surprised to hear the following wafting through the air:

> *Holy Spirit, You are welcome here.*
> *Come flood this place and fill the atmosphere.*
> *Your glory, God, is what our hearts long for,*
> *To be overcome by your presence, Lord.*[18]

Looking around, I realized the sounds were coming from the earphones of a young woman who had her eyes closed and was completely caught up in the music. She didn't realize that all of us in that small room were hearing it as well. At first I was amused, and then I began to ponder: What would it look like if the prayer of her song was answered—not surrounded by other believers in some congregational worship time, but right then and there, where three strangers sat sweating, staring at the floor? What might happen in that place if the Holy Spirit were to fill the atmosphere? Or perhaps more importantly, if I were overwhelmed with God's presence, how might it change the way I view these moments in *my* day?

Living contemplatively means seeing ourselves as harbingers of God's love, ever looking beyond the people and places and events that surround us to what he is doing, how he is working, and how we might have the privilege of joining him. The increasing isolation fostered by our digital worlds makes this hard to do. Let's be honest: In the maelstrom of daily life, we're far more likely to be practicing the presence of our smartphones than contemplating the loving purposes of God. But as David Wells reminds us, "It is in *this* world, not somewhere else, that we must learn to be God-centered in our thoughts and God-honoring in our lives."[19] This requires a discipline no less arduous than that of seeking him in solitude. In short, we need to develop a *present mind*, a *pondering heart*, and a *purposeful will*.

Throughout this book I have addressed our waning powers of attention and how technology trains our minds to flit continually from one thing to the next. Focus, as we've seen, is a dying art. As a spiritual deficiency, this shows up most often in the hubbub of our busy lives. We can be so tethered to technology that we go for hours on end without noticing the kingdom reality that hums along in the background of everything we do. Our continual connections may lull us into assuming we have a *present mind*, but as media theorist Douglas Rushkoff notes, "By dividing our attention between our digital extensions, we sacrifice our connection to the truer present in which we are living."[20] This can be seen in the odd behavior of families or friends who text-message each other rather than talk, even as they sit within arm's reach. It shows up in our habit of broadcasting our lives via tweets or texts or picture posts rather than simply savoring the moments themselves. If we are endlessly enmeshed with our digital devices, how can we hope to hear God's voice or see his hand or grasp his heart for those all around us?

Given our increasing reliance on technology to navigate our worlds, we are going to have to work much harder at having a present mind in order to create space for God. Planning to pull away, even for brief spells throughout the day, is a helpful way to begin. Businessman Peter Bregman suggests that we commit to eighteen minutes a day. He calls for setting aside five minutes in the morning to lay out our day and five minutes in the evening to review it. But his real game changer is to stop for one minute at the top of every hour to ask, *Am I doing what I most need to be doing right now?* and *Am I being who I most want to be right now?*[21] Pondering these kinds of questions before God at least once every hour of the day could be a powerful way to recapture our capacity for contemplative living.

Beyond having a present mind, we need a *pondering heart.* Contemplatives seem to move at a slower pace. They are thoughtful people—they take things in and are in no hurry to speak or act. As a result, they see things others often miss. If we all had eyes to see, we would probably be astonished at how often Jesus desires to reveal his love and compassion through us, feeble though our attempts might be. Daniel Goleman, psychologist and science journalist who wrote the bestselling book *Emotional Intelligence,* notes that when someone is in pain, just the presence of a loving person can have an analgesic effect on the brain's pain center. In fact, the more empathic the ministering person, the greater the calming effect.[22] When we take the time to prayerfully ponder God's heart for the events and people around us, we become that quiet force that changes the very atmosphere as we reach out in the love of Christ.

> IF WE ALL HAD EYES TO SEE, WE WOULD PROBABLY BE ASTONISHED AT HOW OFTEN JESUS DESIRES TO REVEAL HIS LOVE AND COMPASSION THROUGH US.

Living contemplatively may entail something as simple as a smile or a hug, as direct as a prayer or a word of encouragement, or as sacrificial as sabotaging our schedules or emptying out our wallets. But the joy we experience reminds us that we have nothing to lose and everything to gain in giving ourselves away for love. It is perhaps not surprising that acting altruistically appears to trigger the pleasure centers in our brains,[23] something Jesus affirmed long ago when he taught that it is more blessed to give than to receive (Acts 20:35). This joy is what fuels us to have a *purposeful will* in our journey with Jesus throughout the hours of our day.

For me, the choice to act on the Spirit's impressions is not always easy. I tilt at windmills, fearful of giving up control, worried that I haven't heard right or that I might appear foolish or be rejected outright. I know from experience that I tend to make the whole thing a lot more complicated than it really is. Living contemplatively centers on the beautiful truth that we are never alone; the Lover of our souls eagerly awaits to partner with us. The fourteenth-century anonymous author of the classic book on contemplation called *The Cloud of Unknowing* wrote:

> He asks no other help than your own willingness. He wills that you but gaze upon Him and abandon yourself to Him. Keep the windows and doors of your soul against the assailing of outer and inner distraction, both of which hinder His work. If you will do this, you will only reach out to Him meekly with a prayer of love and He will soon help you.[24]

It is such a simple plan—albeit one that requires humility and generosity of soul, as well as the discipline to live in the here and now. With our wills yielded to Christ, we immerse ourselves in each situation—big or small, significant or seemingly insignificant, fleeting or foundational—listening for his gentle and loving guidance. When God speaks, we choose to obey, knowing that the things we do or words that we speak will bring the touch of his very presence—not only for his glory but for our joy.

## The Contemplative Journey

My father has been dead for more than two decades, and yet as I've written this chapter I've felt almost as if he were here cheering me on, for he lived the contemplative journey in an authentic, gritty, down-to-earth way—and he loved every minute of it.

Two images come to mind when I think of my dad's spirituality. The first one greeted me every morning throughout my teenage years as I stumbled out of bed: Dad sitting at the kitchen counter with his Bible open, deep in prayer as he ate his toast and honey and drank his steaming coffee. The second image is of him regularly reaching out to others—stopping the car to fix someone's tire, dropping off a meal or clothes to some needy family, helping a neighbor build a fence, lending a listening ear to someone as he waited in line, or bringing a stranger home for dinner. The list could go on and on, and in fact, on the day before he died, Dad called Mom from the pay phone at the grocery store, asking for their ATM code so he could get some money for a man he'd just met. I learned what "paying it forward" really means from my dad, for inevitably after he'd touched another's life in some way, he would say, "God has blessed us so much; we just want to bless others whenever we can." This was no platitude for Dad: He lived it from the core of his being day in and day out.

This is the contemplative life. We pull away in solitude to let God's love permeate our souls. Then as we go about our day, those experiences of love transform the world before our eyes, and we know why we are here. As a practice, this requires a focus and frame of mind so alien to life in the digital age that we may well find it the most difficult of all to embrace. As Nouwen notes, "To know God in the world requires knowing him by heart. To know God by heart is the purpose of a contemplative discipline. It is a very hard discipline."[25] I want to add, however, that it could well be said that no other discipline nourishes our souls the way that contemplation can. My own experience reminds me that to be infused by a vision of God's love that informs my way of being in this world is life on the highest plane, the smallest taste of a glory that will one day be my eternal reality.

# CONTEMPLATION IN SOLITUDE

ESTIMATED TIME: 30 MINUTES (MINIMUM)

You have said, "Seek my face."
My heart says to you,
    "Your face, LORD, do I seek."

PSALM 27:8

SOME CONFUSION regarding contemplation comes from the fact that the conversation is often about two different things. One is the practice or discipline we engage in to open our hearts up to God, both in solitude and as we live in the world. The other is what we hope to experience when God sovereignly unveils his loving presence to us. Like two sides of a coin, it's impossible to parse out where our part ends and God's begins. But here we will explore some contemplative practices that create space for God and thus increase our capacity for living contemplatively.

To prepare for this time, make sure you are away from all distractions. Put your devices in another room. Have only your Bible and a journal with you.

## Rest

Begin this time either by using God-focused deep breathing (see chapter 4) or by breathing deeply for several minutes as you seek to bring your awareness to this moment and God's presence with you.

Read the following verses slowly and softly once or twice as you seek to let go of distractions, slow down your mind, and enter into a place of rest:

> O LORD, my heart is not lifted up;
>   my eyes are not raised too high;
> I do not occupy myself with things
>   too great and too marvelous for me.

But I have calmed and quieted my soul,
>   like a weaned child with its mother;
>   like a weaned child is my soul within me.

PSALM 131:1-2

For the next five or ten minutes, simply enjoy the reality that God is with you and that you don't have to do anything but rest in his presence. If your mind wanders or you get distracted or feel like you should be "doing something," gently bring your thoughts back to a place of rest without judgment or frustration, knowing that the most important thing you can "do" right now is to just "be" with God. (If you've never done this, you will likely find it very difficult, so be patient with yourself.)

## Reflect

Read the following verses, hearing Jesus speaking them directly to you:

> If anyone loves me, he will keep my word, and my
> Father will love him, and we will come to him and
> make our home with him.

JOHN 14:23

> I will never leave you nor forsake you.

HEBREWS 13:5

Reflect on the reality that God is not far off, that he dwells within you, and that he has made his home in your heart and has promised he will never leave. Envision this and acknowledge it as you place your hand over your heart. Then, for five or ten minutes, picture God's love as a gentle rain softly settling on the soil of your soul. Offer a heart of gratitude and worship without words. Again, if your mind wanders or you get off track, gently return with something like this: "Thank you, Lord, that you are here with me, in me, loving me as I am."

## Resonance

Continuing in a quiet, receptive mode, take five or ten minutes to gently observe the things you have planned for today and the people you might encounter. (If you're doing this at night, look toward tomorrow.) Picture the love that you have experienced here in these moments surrounding you, enveloping you wherever you go, and spilling over to those whose paths you cross. If you find yourself moving into a planning mode or getting distracted by details, simply step back in your mind and receive God's love afresh. Here you simply want to imagine the coming hours as they can be, bathed in the wonder of God's loving plans and purposes.

## Journal

When you have finished, take time to journal about this encounter. Try not to evaluate or assess, but simply write down your feelings and experiences. End by writing a prayer of loving gratitude to the Lord. If you need help, you might begin with these:

Father, because of this time with you, I know \_\_\_\_\_
_____.

Lord, because of this time with you, I am _____
_____.

Jesus, in response to this time with you, I want to
_____.

# CONTEMPLATION IN ACTION

ESTIMATED TIME: 18 MINUTES A DAY FOR 30 DAYS

As for the rich in this present age, charge them not to be haughty, nor to set their hopes on the uncertainty of riches, but on God, who richly provides us with everything to enjoy. They are to do good, to be rich in good works, to be generous and ready to share, thus storing up treasure for themselves as a good foundation for the future, so that they may take hold of that which is truly life.

1 TIMOTHY 6:17-19

THE PURPOSE OF THIS PRACTICE is to get a feel for what it is like to contemplate God's loving purposes as you go through your day. It will involve time in the morning to open your heart to God and time in the evening to express gratitude for his faithfulness. In between, you will be checking in once per hour. You will need some sort of alarm to remind you at the beginning of each hour.

## Morning Watch

If you already spend time with God in the mornings, take the final five minutes of that time for this part of the practice. If you do not have a morning devotional habit, you may want to take some time first just to connect with God and rest in his presence, quieting your heart.

Begin this five-minute session by thanking God for his love for you and offering him your own words of love. Try to let go of all other distractions. Then consider the day before you. What will you be doing? Whom will you be seeing? How will your hours be spent? As you consider these questions, ask God to give you his heart for all of it. Picture him walking with you, his presence there with you every moment. Offer yourself to him, telling him that you desire to commune with him throughout the day. Envision walking out into your day with God as your companion.

## Checking In

Set your smartphone, watch, or computer to remind yourself to pause once per hour throughout the workday. When the reminder comes, take one minute to ask, "Lord, am I being the person you want me to be right now? Lord, is there any way you want me to show your love right now?"

## Evening Watch

Take five minutes before bedtime to consider your contemplative journey with the following questions.

- What difference do I think offering your day to God made?
- How did checking in every hour change things?
- How would I like to grow in this?
- What do I understand more about God's love for me and for others?

Offer a heart of gratitude for God's presence and purpose and for his call for you to be a part of it.

Try to engage in this practice for thirty days in a row in order for it to become a habit and a natural way of life for you.

# A FINAL WORD

TO SAY I'VE NEVER WRITTEN A BOOK like this before would be an understatement. Not only are the topics of brain science and technology well above my pay grade, but the world is changing so fast that I had to continually update as I wrote. (I've no doubt that some of the research I relied upon will be outdated even before the book is released.) Along the way, I often felt like Alice falling down the rabbit hole—curious but completely unprepared for the wild ride, and wondering daily how I ended up here.

Yet undergirding each word there has been a purpose, a passion that fuels not just this book but also everything I have ever written or taught. Simply put, I yearn to see Christ followers fulfill their joyful destiny by walking in intimacy with him. Never have I felt this to be more at risk than today, as the digital revolution alters our very way of being in the world.

As one who is engaged with Christian leaders on a regular basis, it troubles me that it is rare to encounter those whose lives reflect the peaceful presence that comes from meaning-ful communion with Christ in times of solitude and across the byways of life. While people bemoan their busyness and lament the distractions that keep them from practices once considered indispensable for spiritual growth, few express alarm about it. Indeed, there seems to be an almost fatalistic assumption that we have no control over the feverish pace that drives our lives.

My prayer is that as you have read and begun to engage the practices in this book, you've gleaned new insights and experienced fresh hope for your own journey with Jesus. I hope these have spurred you to be more resolute about not surrendering control of your life to the demands of your digi-tal devices or the exigencies of a tech-saturated culture.

Because Jesus Christ is the same yesterday, today, and for-ever, be assured that he is committed to helping you navigate your hyperconnected worlds so that you can experience life to its fullest measure. As you walk with him through the minefield of an ever-changing digital landscape, may you move a little slower, ponder a little longer, and connect a little deeper. May you be relentless about creating space—space to see Christ's beauty and experience his love, and space for your light to shine brighter with his glory.

# ACKNOWLEDGMENTS

I AM SO GRATEFUL for the people God has put in my life to walk with me through the arduous writing process. My agent and friend, Steve Laube, expanded my vision for this book when it was only a seed germinating in my heart. He also coined the phrase "wired soul" in our very first conversation, because he really did get it. I have been so blessed by his insights and support for over two decades.

It has been a delight to work with NavPress on this project. Thanks to publisher Don Pape and the Tyndale alliance for seeing the potential and taking the risk. Jen and Dean did a great job capturing the nuances of a complex topic for the cover. Most of all, my gratitude goes to David Zimmerman, an astute editor whose careful attention has made the book so much better. I would never want to write without the backup of an editor like David.

Many friends and family have stood by me, eagerly cheering me on this past year. New Hope Church's continual encouragement has sustained me more than they will ever know. Of course, the one person I could not have done without is my husband of forty-two years, Joe Rhodes. He has been my chief theologian, my first-read editor, and an incredible sounding board and cheerleader. I cannot say enough.

Finally, and most importantly, I give thanks to God, who continually surprises me with his call and whose love is the impetus behind every word I write.

# NOTES

## CHAPTER 1: WIRED SOULS IN A DIGITAL WORLD

1. "Digital native" and "digital immigrant" are terms coined by author Marc Prensky. They have become a part of the cultural jargon regarding the technological revolution. He explains: "Digital Immigrants lived in two cultures: the pre-digital and the digital. Digital Natives have known only the digital culture. A great many of the Digital Immigrants' deeply-felt attitudes and preferences were formed in, and reflect, the pre-digital culture and age." Mark Prensky, "Digital Natives," accessed September 1, 2015, http://marcprensky.com/digital-native/.

2. Douglas Rushkoff, *Present Shock: When Everything Happens Now* (New York: Current, 2013), 87.

3. This is called the Hebbian theory or Hebb's Law, after Dr. Donald Hebb, a neuropsychologist who combined the study of human behavior with brain science. He summarized his findings in the book *The Organization of Behavior: A Neuropsychological Theory* (New York: John Wiley and Sons, 1949). The actual principle is stated in the book as follows: "When an axon of cell A is near enough to excite cell B and repeatedly or persistently takes part in firing it, some growth process or metabolic change takes place in one or both cells such that A's efficiency, as one of the cells firing B, is increased."

4. Maggie Jackson, *Distracted: The Erosion of Attention and the Coming Dark Age* (Amherst, NY: Prometheus Books, 2009), 22, 252; Judith Horstman, *The Scientific American Day in the Life of Your Brain* (San Francisco: Jossey-Bass, 2009); Andrew Newberg and Mark Robert Waldman, *How God Changes Your Brain: Breakthrough Findings from a Leading Neuroscientist* (New York: Ballantine, 2009).

5. *Lectio divina,* or sacred reading, seems to have begun with Saint Benedict

as part of his Rule, which involved both individual and corporate reading of biblical passages over and over, with a goal of experiencing the presence of God. In the twelfth century a Carthusian monk named Guigo II wrote a letter to another monk with a treatise on prayer that he called "the Ladder of Monks." It incorporated four steps of growth—*lectio, meditatio, oratio,* and *contemplatio.* In the twentieth century, the Second Vatican Council recommended *lectio divina* for the general public; its practice has since become widespread across many Christian groups, both Catholic and Protestant.

6. I am using each of these four components of *lectio divina* as separate metaphors to represent the kinds of growth desired and the practices that can aid in it. I am thankful to Maria Lichtmann and her book *The Teacher's Way: Teaching and the Contemplative Life* (Mahwah, NJ: Paulist, 2005) for this idea.

### CHAPTER 2: SLOW READING AND DEEP THINKING

1. Data regarding Americans' use of time for the years 2003–2014 can be found at the Bureau of Labor Statistics, "American Time Use Survey," accessed February 24, 2016, www.bls.gov/tus/. There have been numerous other studies over the past decade with similar findings. Statistics in this book are from studies by the Kaiser Family Foundation and the National Education Association, cited by Michael Harris in his book *The End of Absence: Reclaiming What We've Lost in a World of Constant Connection* (New York: Current, 2014). It should also be noted here that some suggest that activity on the Internet constitutes reading, and as such it is not being taken into account in these kinds of statistics.

2. See, for example, Mark Bauerlein, *The Dumbest Generation: How the Digital Age Stupefies Young Americans and Jeopardizes Our Future* (New York: Penguin, 2008); and Nicholas Carr, "Is Google Making Us Stupid?" Yearbook of the National Society for the Study of Education 107, no. 2 (2008), 89–94.

3. Maryanne Wolf, "Our 'Deep Reading' Brain: Its Digital Evolution Poses Questions," Summer 2010, accessed September 1, 2015, at http://niemanreports.org/articles/our-deep-reading-brain-its-digital-evolution-poses-questions/.

4. Carr, "Is Google Making Us Stupid?" 89.

5. See C. Christopher Smith and John Pattison, *Slow Church: Cultivating Community in the Patient Way of Jesus* (Downers Grove, IL: InterVarsity, 2014).

6. For an overview of the various facets of this loose group of organizations, see www.slowmovement.com/aboutus.php, accessed September 1, 2015.

7. David Mikics, *Slow Reading in a Hurried Age* (Cambridge, MA: Belknap Press, 2013), 6.

8. Harper Lee, *To Kill a Mockingbird* (Philadelphia: Lippincott, 1960), 30.

9. Thomas Newkirk, *The Art of Slow Reading: Six Time-Honored Practices for Engagement* (Portsmouth, NH: Heinemann, 2011), 6.

10. C. S. Lewis, *An Experiment in Criticism* (Cambridge: University Press, 1961), 141.

11. Sven Birkerts, *The Gutenberg Elegies: The Fate of Reading in an Electronic Age* (Boston: Faber and Faber, 1994), 75.

12. According to a 2012 survey by the Pew Research Center, 58 percent of Millennials say they cannot be certain that God exists, as opposed to 69 percent of Gen-Xers and 73 percent of baby boomers. For the full study, see "Millennials in Adulthood," March 7, 2014, www.pewsocialtrends.org/2014/03/07/millennials-in-adulthood/.

## CHAPTER 3: EAT THIS BOOK

1. Annual Bible usage research conducted by the Barna Group in conjunction with the American Bible Society. See American Bible Society, "State of the Bible 2015," accessed September 2, 2015, www.americanbible.org/features/state-of-the-bible-research-2014.

2. See Barna Group, "The State of the Bible: Six Trends for 2014," April 8, 2014, accessed September 2, 2015, www.barna.org/barna-update/culture/664-the-state-of-the-bible-6-trends-for-2014.

3. See Barna Group, "Millennials and the Bible: Three Surprising Insights," October 21, 2014, accessed September 2, 2015, at www.barna.org/barna-update/millennials/687-millennials-and-the-bible-3-surprising-insights.

4. Stanislas Dehaene, *Reading in the Brain: The New Science of How We Read* (New York: Penguin, 2010), 2.

5. Alex Murashko, "Bible App 5 Shows YouVersion Still on Track to Engage the World in Scripture," April 23, 2014, www.christianpost.com/news/bible-app-5-shows-youversion-still-on-track-to-engage-the-world-in-scripture-118434/.

6. See American Bible Society, "State of the Bible 2015."

7. David Wells, *God in the Whirlwind: How the Holy-Love of God Reorients Our World* (Wheaton, IL: Crossway, 2014), 17–18.

8. Wells, *God in the Whirlwind*, 37–38.

9. Eugene Peterson, *Eat This Book: A Conversation in the Art of Spiritual Reading* (Grand Rapids, MI: Eerdmans, 2009), 10.

10. Wells, *God in the Whirlwind*.

11. Augustine, quoted in Thomas Newkirk, *The Art of Slow Reading: Six Time-Honored Practices for Engagement* (Portsmouth, NH: Heinemann, 2012), 76, emphasis added. The word *lime* is an old English term referring to a substance used in plasters, mortars, and cements; thus Augustine was speaking of "cementing" something into our memory.

12. Andrew Newberg and Mark Robert Waldman, *How God Changes Your Brain: Breakthrough Findings from a Leading Neuroscientist* (New York: Ballantine, 2009).

13. Ian Burrell, "Inside Google HQ," July 19, 2013, www.independent.co.uk /life-style/gadgets-and-tech/features/inside-google-hq-what-does-the-future -hold-for-the-company-whose-visionary-plans-include-implanting -8714487.html.

14. Thomas Newkirk, *The Art of Slow Reading: Six Time-Honored Practices for Engagement* (Portsmouth, NH: Heinemann, 2011), 77.

15. Dallas Willard, "Spiritual Formation in Christ for the Whole Life and the Whole Person," *Vocatio* 12, no. 2 (Spring 2001), 7.

16. Psalm 1:1-6; 37:21; 40:8; 119:11, 16; Proverbs 6:21-22; Matthew 4:4.

**CHAPTER 4: MAY I HAVE YOUR ATTENTION, PLEASE?**

1. Maggie Jackson, *Distracted: The Erosion of Attention and the Coming Dark Age* (Amherst, NY: Prometheus Books, 2009), 14.

2. Douglas Groothuis, quoted in Tony Reinke, "Six Ways Your Phone Is Changing You," July 19, 2014, www.desiringgod.org/articles/six-ways -your-phone-is-changing-you.

3. Richard Foster, *Sanctuary of the Soul: Journey into Meditative Prayer* (Downers Grove, IL: InterVarsity, 2011).

4. There are various apps that use the camera lens to allow a person to read and walk at the same time. For a description of one called Type n Walk, see Ellie Zolfagharifard, "Text AND Walk," March 4, 2014, www.dailymail .co.uk/sciencetech/article-2573087/Text-AND-walk-App-makes-mobile -transparent-street-typing.html.

5. Steve Bradt, "Wandering Mind Not a Happy Mind," November 11, 2010, accessed November 6, 2015, at http://news.harvard.edu/gazette/story/2010 /11/wandering-mind-not-a-happy-mind/.

6. Ruth Haley Barton, *Invitation to Solitude and Silence: Experiencing God's Transforming Presence* (Downers Grove, IL: InterVarsity, 2004).

7. Evelyn Underhill, *Practical Mysticism* (Boston: E. P. Dutton and Company,

1915), accessed September 2, 2015, at www.gutenberg.org/files/21774 /21774-h/21774-h.htm#5.

8. Daniel G. Amen, *The Amen Solution: The Brain Healthy Way to Lose Weight and Keep It Off* (New York: Crown Archetype, 2011).

9. Taken from the *Philokalia*, a collection of texts from the Orthodox tradition, written between the fourth and fifteenth century and compiled in the eighteenth century. Accessed September 2, 2015, at https://archive .org/stream/Philokalia-TheCompleteText/Philokalia-Complete-Text#page /n1017/mode/2up.

10. Elder Mullan, trans., *The Spiritual Exercises of St. Ignatius of Loyola* (New York: P. J. Kennedy and Sons, 1914), accessed September 2, 2015, at www .sacred-texts.com/chr/seil/index.htm.

11. Morton T. Kelsey, *The Other Side of Silence: A Guide to Christian Meditation* (Mahwah, NJ: Paulist, 1976), 111.

12. Andrew Newberg and Mark Robert Waldman, *How God Changes Your Brain: Breakthrough Findings from a Leading Neuroscientist* (New York: Ballantine, 2009).

13. Sondra Kornblatt, *A Better Brain at Any Age* (San Francisco: Conari, 2008).

14. Newberg and Waldman, *How God Changes Your Brain*, 33.

## CHAPTER 5: MEDITATION—THE LABORATORY OF THE SOUL

1. Martin Heidegger, *Discourse on Thinking: A Translation of Gelassenheit* (New York: Harper Perennial, 2000), 56, emphasis added.

2. Nicholas Carr, *The Shallows: What the Internet Is Doing to Our Brains* (New York: W.W. Norton, 2010).

3. Hebrew Lexicon: H1897 and H7878 (ESV), accessed September 2, 2015, at www.blueletterbible.org/lang/lexicon/lexicon.cfm?Strongs=H1897&t=ESV.

4. Psalm 63:6; 77:12; 143:5; 145:5.

5. Andrew Newberg and Mark Robert Waldman, *How God Changes Your Brain: Breakthrough Findings from a Leading Neuroscientist* (New York: Ballantine, 2009), 5-6.

6. Greek Lexicon: G3563 (ESV), accessed September 2, 2015, at www .blueletterbible.org/lang/lexicon/lexicon.cfm?Strongs=G3563&t=ESV.

7. Morton T. Kelsey, *The Other Side of Silence: A Guide to Christian Meditation* (Mahwah, NJ: Paulist, 1976), 9.

8. Richard Foster, *Sanctuary of the Soul: Journey into Meditative Prayer* (Downers Grove, IL: IVP Books, 2011), 26.

9. Joshua 1:8; Psalm 63:5-6; Isaiah 26:3; Romans 8:6.

10. Newberg and Waldman, *How God Changes Your Brain*, 16.

11. See Newberg and Waldman, *How God Changes Your Brain*; Sondra Kornblatt, *A Better Brain at Any Age* (San Francisco: Conari, 2008); and Daniel Bor, *The Ravenous Brain: How the New Science of Consciousness Explains Our Insatiable Search for Meaning* (New York: Basic Books, 2012).

12. See my chapter on meditative prayer in Tricia Rhodes, *The Soul at Rest: A Journey into Contemplative Prayer* (Minneapolis: Bethany House, 1996), and the chapter on meditation in Richard Foster, *A Celebration of Discipline: The Path to Spiritual Growth* (San Francisco: Harper & Row, 1988).

13. Curt Thompson, *Anatomy of the Soul: Surprising Connections between Neuroscience and Spiritual Practices That Can Transform Your Life and Relationships* (Carol Stream, IL: SaltRiver, 2010).

14. Eugene Peterson, *Eat This Book: A Conversation in the Art of Spiritual Reading* (Grand Rapids, MI: Eerdmans, 2009).

15. Hans Urs von Balthasar, *Prayer* (New York: Sheed & Ward, 1961), 35.

16. Peterson, *Eat This Book,* 59.

17. Thompson, *Anatomy of the Soul,* 48.

### CHAPTER 6: PRAYING THE TEXTS OF OUR DIGITAL LIVES

1. James K. A. Smith, *Desiring the Kingdom: Worship, Worldview, and Cultural Formation* (Grand Rapids, MI: Baker Academic, 2009), 23. Smith uses the word *apocalyptic* here because the purpose of apocalyptic literature, such as the book of Revelation, was to provide a Godward vision to counter that of cultural institutions and practices of the day. He calls for "a contemporary apocalyptic—a language and a genre that sees through the spin and unveils for us the religious and idolatrous character of the contemporary institutions that constitute our own milieu" (p. 92).

2. Elise Hu, "New Numbers Back Up Our Obsession with Phones," *All Tech Considered,* October 10, 2013, www.npr.org/sections/alltechconsidered/2013/10/09/230867952/new-numbers-back-up-our-obsession-with-phones.

3. Jaron Lanier, "Fixing the Digital Economy," *New York Times,* June 8, 2013, www.nytimes.com/2013/06/09/opinion/sunday/fixing-the-digital-economy.html?_r=0. See also Jaron Lanier, "Digital Passivity," *New York Times,* November 27, 2013, www.nytimes.com/2013/11/28/opinion/digital-passivity.html?_r=1.

4. See Douglas Groothuis, "Christian Scholarship and the Philosophical Analysis of Cyberspace Technologies," *Journal of the Evangelical Theological Society* 41, no. 4 (1998), 633.

5. Tony Reinke, "Six Ways Your iPhone Is Changing You," *Desiring God* (blog), July 19, 2014, www.desiringgod.org/articles/six-ways-your-phone -is-changing-you, emphasis added.

### CHAPTER 7: ALONE . . . TOGETHER

1. Mark Zuckerberg, Facebook post, March 25, 2014, accessed September 2, 2015, at www.facebook.com/zuck/posts/10101319050523971?pnref=story.

2. Douglas Groothuis, "Christian Scholarship and the Philosophical Analysis of Cyberspace Technologies," *Journal of the Evangelical Theological Society* 41, no. 4 (1998): 638–639.

3. See Curt Thompson, *Anatomy of the Soul: Surprising Connections between Neuroscience and Spiritual Practices That Can Transform Your Life and Relationships* (Carol Stream, IL: SaltRiver, 2010).

4. Leonard Sweet, *From Tablet to Table: Where Community Is Found and Identity Is Formed* (Colorado Springs: NavPress, 2015), 33.

5. Thompson, *Anatomy of the Soul*, 24.

6. Sherry Turkle, *Alone Together: Why We Expect More from Technology and Less from Each Other* (New York: Basic Books, 2011), 16.

7. Jun Young and David Kinnaman, *The Hyperlinked Life: Live with Wisdom in an Age of Information Overload* (Grand Rapids, MI: Zondervan, 2013).

8. Turkle, *Alone Together*, 17.

9. Tony Reinke, "Smartphone Addiction and Our Spiritual ADD," *Desiring God* (blog), April 18, 2015, www.desiringgod.org/articles/smartphone -addiction-and-our-spiritual-add.

10. James K. A. Smith, *Desiring the Kingdom: Worship, Worldview, and Cultural Formation* (Grand Rapids, MI: Baker Academic, 2009).

11. Reinke, "Smartphone Addiction and Our Spiritual ADD."

12. *Strong's Exhaustive Concordance* defines *koinonia* as "partnership, i.e. (literally) participation, or (social) intercourse, or (pecuniary) benefaction—(to) communicate(-ation), communion, (contri-) distribution, fellowship." Accessed October 13, 2015, at http://biblehub. com/strongs/greek/2842.htm.

13. James K. A. Smith, *Desiring the Kingdom: Worship, Worldview, and Cultural Formation* (Grand Rapids, MI: Baker Academic, 2009), 211.

14. Reinke, "Smartphone Addiction and Our Spiritual ADD."

15. Sweet, *From Tablet to Table*, 19.

16. Sweet, *From Tablet to Table*, 67.

**CHAPTER 8: THE CONTEMPLATIVE LIFE**

1. See Mark Galli and Ted Olsen, ed. *131 Christians Everyone Should Know* (Nashville: Broadman & Holman, 2000).

2. "Finding God in All Things," accessed September 2, 2015, at http://jesuits .org/spirituality.

3. Richard Foster, *Prayer: Finding the Heart's True Home* (New York: HarperCollins, 1992), 156.

4. Eugene Peterson, *Eat This Book: A Conversation in the Art of Spiritual Reading* (Grand Rapids, MI: Eerdmans, 2009), 113.

5. In my first book, *The Soul at Rest: A Journey into Contemplative Prayer* (Minneapolis: Bethany House, 1996), I took the same view as Richard Foster and dozens of other spiritual writers, describing contemplation as a form of prayer that we must be spiritually prepared to undertake. The view is rooted in the practices of mystics who seek to spend hours in silent contemplation, something most of us are probably not prone to do. I have since revised my understanding, as this chapter explains.

6. As explained in Henri Nouwen's *Clowning in Rome: Reflections on Solitude, Celibacy, Prayer, and Contemplation* (New York: Image, 1979), 88, 97.

7. Thomas DuBay, *Fire Within: St. Teresa of Avila, St. John of the Cross, and the Gospel—on Prayer* (San Francisco: Ignatius Press, 1989), 61.

8. DuBay, *Fire Within*, 57.

9. Peterson, *Eat This Book*, 113.

10. Nouwen, *Clowning in Rome*, 15.

11. Augustine, "Sermon 8 on the First Commandment," as cited in Benignus O'Rourke, *Finding Your Hidden Treasure: The Way of Silent Prayer* (Andrews, UK: Liguori, 2013), 18.

12. Paul Fromont, "Rowan Williams on Prayer," December 23, 2008, accessed September 3, 2015, at http://prodigal.typepad.com/prodigal_kiwi/2008 /12/rowan-williams-on-prayer.html.

13. Marva Dawn, *A Royal "Waste" of Time: The Splendor of Worshiping God and Being Church for the World* (Grand Rapids, MI: Eerdmans, 1999), 11.

14. Nouwen, *Clowning in Rome*, 28.

15. Saint Augustine, "On John's Gospel," as cited in O'Rourke, *Finding Your Hidden Treasure*, 11.

16. See "In the Garden," accessed September 3, 2015, at www.tanbible.com /tol_sng/sng_inthegarden.htm.

17. Sven Birkerts, *The Gutenberg Elegies: The Fate of Reading in an Electronic Age* (New York: Faber and Faber, 1994), 76.

18. The song, it turns out, was "Holy Spirit," lyrics and music by Katie Torwalt and Bryan Torwalt, *Jesus Culture*, 2015.

19. David Wells, *God in the Whirlwind: How the Holy-Love of God Reorients Our World* (Wheaton, IL: Crossway, 2014), 37.

20. Douglas Rushkoff, *Present Shock: When Everything Happens Now* (New York: Current, 2013), 75.

21. Peter Bregman, *Eighteen Minutes: Find Your Focus, Master Distraction, and Get the Right Things Done* (New York: Business Plus, 2011).

22. Daniel Goleman, *Emotional Intelligence* (New York: Bantam, 1995), 108.

23. Sondra Kornblatt, *A Better Brain at Any Age* (San Francisco: Conari, 2008), 151.

24. In Evelyn Underhill, *A Book of Contemplation: The Which Is Called the Cloud of Unknowing, in the Which a Soul Is Oned with God* (London: J. M. Watkins, 1956).

25. Nouwen, *Clowning in Rome*, 105.

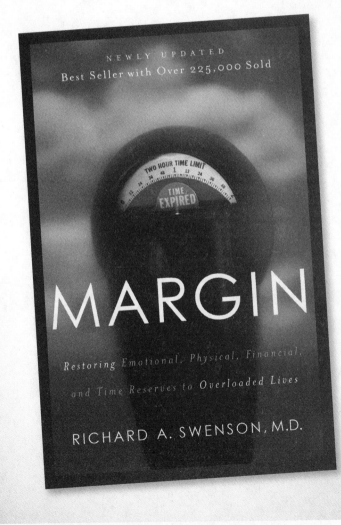

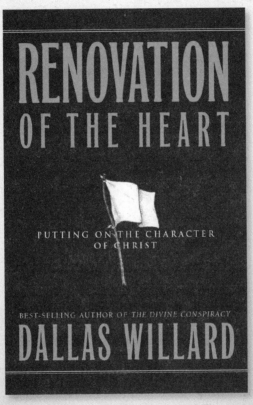